OF SPIRIT

HEIDEGGER AND THE QUESTION

JACQUES DERRIDA

TRANSLATED BY
GEOFFREY BENNINGTON
AND RACHEL BOWLBY

THE UNIVERSITY OF
CHICAGO PRESS

Chicago and London

JACQUES DERRIDA is professor at the Ecole des
Hautes Etudes en Sciences Sociales, Paris, and holds visiting
professorships at the University of California, Irvine, and at
Cornell University.

GEOFFREY BENNINGTON, lecturer in French in the
School of European Studies at the University of Sussex, is the
cotranslator of Jean-François Lyotard's *The Postmodern
Condition.*

RACHEL BOWLBY, lecturer in English at the University
of Sussex, is the author of *Just Looking* and *Virginia Woolf:
Feminist Destinations.*

Originally published as *De l'esprit,*
© Editions Galilée, 1987

The University of Chicago Press, Chicago 60637
The University of Chicago Press, Ltd., London
© 1989 by The University of Chicago
All rights reserved. Published 1989
Printed in the United States of America

98 97 96 95 94 93 92 91 90 89   5 4 3 2 1

⊛ The paper used in this publication meets the
minimum requirements of the American
National Standard for Information Sciences—
Permanence of Paper for Printed Library
Materials, ANSI Z39.48-1984.

Library of Congress Cataloging-in-Publication Data

Derrida, Jacques
  [De l'esprit. English]
  Of spirit : Heidegger and the question / Jacques Derrida :
translated by Geoffrey Bennington and Rachel Bowlby.
     p. cm.
  Translation of: De l'esprit.
  Bibliography: p.
  ISBN 0-226-14317-1 (alk. paper).
    1. Heidegger, Martin, 1889–1976. I. Title.
B3279.H49D4813   1989
  193—dc19   88-32212
                                                      CIP

CONTENTS

TRANSLATORS' NOTE
vii

CHAPTER I
1

CHAPTER II
7

CHAPTER III
14

CHAPTER IV
23

CHAPTER V
31

CHAPTER VI
47

CHAPTER VII
58

CHAPTER VIII
73

CHAPTER IX
83

CONTENTS

CHAPTER X
99

NOTES
115

TRANSLATORS' NOTE

The text translated here is that of a lecture given 14 March 1987 at the end of a conference organized by the Collège international de philosophie in Paris, entitled "Heidegger: Open Questions." The notes were naturally added later. We give references wherever possible to English translations of the texts by Heidegger cited by Jacques Derrida. We have benefited from being able to consult these translations, but have retranslated throughout in the interests of consistency and proximity to the versions used by Derrida.

I

I shall speak of ghost [*revenant*], of flame, and of ashes.
And of what, for Heidegger, *avoiding* means.

What is avoiding? Heidegger on several occasions uses the common word *vermeiden:* to avoid, to flee, to dodge. What might he have meant when it comes to "spirit" or the "spiritual"? I specify immediately: not spirit or the spiritual but *Geist, geistig, geistlich*, for this question will be, through and through, that of language. Do these German words allow themselves to be translated? In another sense: are they avoidable?

Sein und Zeit (1927): what does Heidegger say at that time? He announces and he prescribes. He *warns* [*avertit*]: a certain number of terms will have to be avoided (*vermeiden*). Among them, spirit (*Geist*). In 1953, more than twenty-five years later—and this was not just any quarter-century—in the great text devoted to Trakl, Heidegger notes that Trakl always took care to avoid (*vermeiden* again) the word *geistig*. And, visibly, Heidegger approves him in this, he thinks the same. But this time, it is not *Geist* nor even *geistlich* which is to be avoided, but *geistig*.

How are we to delimit the difference, and what has happened? What of this meantime? How are we to explain that in twenty-five years, between these two *warning* signals ("avoid," "avoid using"), Heidegger made a frequent, regular, marked (if not remarked) use of all this vocabulary, including the adjective *geistig*? And that he often spoke not only of the word "spirit" but, sometimes yielding to the emphatic mode, in the name of spirit?

Could it be that he failed to avoid what he knew he ought to avoid? What he in some sense had promised himself to avoid? Could it be that he forgot to avoid? Or else, as one might suspect, are things more tortuous and entangled than this?

Here one could get into writing a chapter destined for a different book. I imagine its title: "How to Avoid Speaking."[1] What does "avoid" mean, in particular in Heidegger?—and it is not necessarily avoidance or denegation. These latter categories are insufficient insofar as the discourse which habitually puts them to work, that of psychoanalysis for example, does not take into account the economy of *vermeiden* in those places where it exposes itself to the question of Being. The least one can say is that we are very far away from this taking into account. And all I should like to attempt here is to approach it. I'm thinking in particular of all those modalities of "avoiding" which come down to saying without saying, writing without writing, using words without using them: in quotation marks, for example, under a non-negative cross-shaped crossing out (*kreuzweise Durchstreichung*), or again in propositions of the type: "If I were yet to write a theology, as I am sometimes tempted to do, the word 'Being' ought not to appear in it,"[2] etc. Now we know well enough that, at the date at which he said that, Heidegger had already made this word disappear while allowing it to appear under a crossing-out—which had thus perhaps set him going, and a long time since, on the path of that theology he says he would only like to write but which he does not *not* write at this very point, saying it's not that at all, saying that that's the last thing he's doing and that he would have to shut up his thinking-shop if one day he were to be called by the faith.[3] In saying this, is he not showing that he can do it? And that he could easily, even, be the only one who could do it?

The title which imposed itself upon me for this lecture might have surprised or shocked some of you, whether or not they recognized the quotation—this time without parody—of a scandalous book, originally anonymous and consigned to the fire.[4]

This title appears today to be anachronistic in its grammar and its diction, as if it took us back to the age when they still wrote systematic treatises on the model of Latin compositions in the Ciceronian style (*De spiritu*), when what is called French materialism of the eighteenth century or French spiritualism of following centuries established on this model the finest canons of our school rhetoric. The anachronistic form, or even the provocatively "retro" character of this *Of Spirit* seems even more bizarre in the landscape of this conference, for reasons both of style (nothing in it recalls a Heideggerian manner) and, if I can say this, of semantics: spirit, so it seems at least, is not a great word of Heidegger's. It is not his theme. It would seem that he was able, precisely, to avoid it. And who would dare to suspect in him that metaphysics—materialist or spiritualist—which produced the great days and best moments of a French tradition, the very tradition which has so durably marked our philosophical institutions?

Because this suspicion appears absurd, because it carries in it something intolerable, and perhaps too because it moves towards the most worrying places in Heidegger's itinerary, discourses, and history, people avoid in their turn speaking *of spirit* in a work which nonetheless lets itself be magnetized, from its first to its last word, by that very thing.

Is it not remarkable that this theme, spirit, occupying—as I hope to show in a minute that it does—a major and obvious place in this line of thought, should have been disinherited [*forclos d'héritage*]? No one wants anything to do with it any more, in the entire family of Heideggerians, be they the orthodox or the heretical, the neo-Heideggerians or the para-Heideggerians, the disciples or the experts. No one ever speaks of spirit in Heidegger. Not only this: even the anti-Heideggerian specialists take no interest in this thematics of spirit, not even to denounce it. Why? What is going on? What is being avoided by this? Why this filtering out in the heritage, and this discrimination? Why even when the legacy is being rejected does *Geist* not occupy the place it deserves alongside the major themes and major terms: being, *Dasein*, time, the world, history, ontological difference, *Ereignis*, etc.?

It was perhaps necessary to run the risk of a classical academicism so as to mark, while yet leaving it open—for it is not my intention to deal with it—the French dimension, the Franco-German chronicle in which we are *situating* Heidegger during this conference which was also an *Erörterung* keeping the questions "open," in view of this place. *De l'esprit* is a thoroughly French title, much too French to give the sense of the *geistige* or *geistliche* of *Geist*. But that is the point: it will perhaps be heard better in German. Perhaps, at any rate, we will be more properly sensitive to its Germanness if we let its resonance be heard coming from a foreign language, so as to put it to the test of translation, or rather if we put to the test its resistance to translation. And if we submit our own language to the same test.

This necessity remains on one side. I will not rely for the essential justification of my topic on an introduction or preface. Here, nonetheless, are *three* preliminary arguments.

There is first the necessity of this essential *explanation*, the quarrel between languages, German *and* Rome, German *and* Latin, and even German *and* Greek, the *Übersetzung* as *Auseinandersetzung* between *pneuma*, *spiritus*, and *Geist*. At a certain point, this last no longer allows of translation into the first two. "Tell me what you think about translation and I will tell you who you are," recalls Heidegger on the subject of Sophocles' *Antigone*.[5] In this title *De l'esprit*, the Franco-Latin *de* also announces that, in the classical form of the enquiry, and even of the dissertation, I wish to begin to treat *of spirit*—the word and the concept, the terms *Geist, geistig, geistlich*—in Heidegger. I shall begin to follow modestly the itineraries, the functions, the formations and regulated transformations, the presuppositions and the destinations. This preliminary work has not yet been systematically undertaken—to my knowledge, perhaps not even envisaged. Such a silence is not without significance. It does not derive only from the fact that, although the lexicon of spirit is more copious in Heidegger than is thought, he never made it the title or the principal theme of an extended meditation, a book, a seminar, or even a lecture. And yet—I will attempt to show this—what thereby remains unquestioned in the invocation of *Geist* by Heidegger is, more than a *coup de force*, force *itself* in its most out-of-the-ordinary manifestation. This motif of spirit or of the spiritual acquires an extraordinary authority *in its German language*. To the precise extent that it does not appear at the forefront of the scene, it seems to withdraw itself from any destruction or deconstruction, as if it did not belong to a history of ontology—and the problem will be just that.

On the other hand, and this is a second argument, this motif is regularly inscribed in contexts that are highly charged politically, in the moments when thought lets itself be preoccupied more than ever by what is called history, language, the nation, *Geschlecht*, the Greek or German languages. From this lexicon, which we are not justified in calling spiritualist or even spiritual—can I risk saying *spirituelle?*—Heidegger draws abundantly in the years 1933–35, above all in the *Rectorship Address* and the *Introduction to Metaphysics*, and also in a different way in *Nietzsche*. But during the following twenty years, and except for one inflection which I will try to analyze, this same lexicon gives direction for example to the seminars and writings on Schelling, Hölderlin, and especially Trakl. In them it even takes on a thematic value which is not without a certain novelty.

Here finally is my third preliminary argument: if the thinking of *Geist* and of the difference between *geistig* and *geistlich* is neither thematic nor athematic and if its modality thus requires another category, then it is not only inscribed in contexts with a high political content, as I have just said rapidly and rather conventionally. It perhaps decides as to the very meaning of the political as such. In any case it would situate the place of such a decision, if it were possible. Whence its privilege, still scarcely visible, for what are called the questions of the political or of politics which are stimulating so many debates around Heidegger today—doubtless in renewed form in France, thanks notably to Lacoue-Labarthe—at the point at which they tie up with the great questions of Being and truth, of history, of the *Ereignis*, of the thought and unthought or, for I always prefer to say this in the plural, the thoughts and the unthoughts of Heidegger.

II

Open Questions: I recall the subtitle proposed for this conference. Before really beginning, I must say a few words about what, today, are for me the *open questions*—questions opened by Heidegger and open with regard to Heidegger. This will permit me to describe the economy or strategy which imposed the choice of this theme on me today, at a certain point in my reading, at a moment which is no doubt for me that of the greatest hesitation and the gravest perplexity. These few remarks, however preliminary they still remain, will perhaps illuminate the path I shall follow.

This attention paid to *Geist,* which recently gave me my direction in some readings of Hegel,[1] is today called forth by research I have been pursuing for a few years now in a seminar on philosophical nationality and nationalism. Often enough in this research, it is certain texts of Heidegger's which constitute the test case itself. These texts are also under test, especially when it is a question of language and of place. While pursuing the work to which I had published a short preface under the title "Geschlecht, différence sexuelle, différence ontologique,"[2] I attempted to follow the trace and the stakes of *Geschlecht,* that frighteningly polysemic and practically untranslatable word (race, lineage, stock, generation, sex) in the text on Trakl from *Unterwegs zur Sprache.* Now in this text one encounters a distinction which Heidegger would like to be of decisive importance, between *geistig* and *geistlich,* and then a singular divide right inside the word *geistlich.* Naturally I intend to return

7

to this distinction and this divide which organize the thinking of *Geschlecht* at this point on Heidegger's path.

On the other hand, still within the same seminar, a reading, as patient as possible, of the *Timaeus*—and especially of what relates to the *chora* in it, seemed to me to render at least problematical the interpretation of it that Heidegger puts forward in the *Introduction to Metaphysics.* Other questions could then be deployed and articulated among themselves on the basis of this example. These questions concern the general interpretation of the history of onto-theology or what I shall call, using a word which Heidegger would have refused and which I myself use for provisional convenience, the *axiomatics* of *Destruktion* and of the epochal schema in general. But the use of this word, *axiomatics*, is suspect only from the point of view of this epochal schema itself. So one is not obliged to forbid oneself in advance what Heidegger prescribes that one proscribe. Why not stand firm and interrogate this prescription and this proscription?

Last year, in preparation for another conference on Heidegger, at the University of Essex (David Krell, who is among us today, organized it and some of you were there), I held at Yale a sort of private seminar with some American friends.[3] In replying to their questions or suggestions, I tried to define what appeared to me to be left hanging, uncertain, still in movement and therefore, for me at least, *yet to come* in Heidegger's text. I distinguished four guiding threads, and at the end of this conversation, which I reported to the Essex conference, I had to ask myself: what ties together these four threads? What interlaces them? What is the knot of this *Geflecht*, if, that is, there is one, a single simple knot, which is never certain—and this is, even, the ultimate or the always penultimate question.

Now here is the hypothesis I want to put to the test today by submitting it to you. Following the trace of Heidegger's spirituality would perhaps approach, not a central point of this knot—I believe there is none—but approach what gathers a nodal resistance in its most economical torsion. I shall explain in conclusion why what I am presenting politely as a hypothesis must necessarily turn out to be true. I know that this hypothesis is true, as though in advance. Its verification appears to me to be as paradoxical as it is fated. At stake in it is the truth of truth for Heidegger, a truth the tautology of which does not even have to be discovered or invented. It belongs to the beyond and to the possibility of any question, to the unquestionable itself in any question. *Geist* cannot fail to gather this interlacing insofar as, for Heidegger, as we shall verify, it is another name for the One and the *Versammlung*, one of the names of collecting and gathering.

The first of the four threads leads, precisely, to the *question*, to the question of the question, to the apparently absolute and long unquestioned privilege of the *Fragen*—of, in the last instance, the essentially questioning form, essence and dignity of thought or the path of thought. There are indeed moments, as we shall see, when Heidegger differentiates the modes of *questioning, asking* or *interrogating*, even analyzing the reflexive repetition of such and such a question: "why 'why'?" But, it seems to me, he *almost* never stopped identifying what is highest and best in thought with the question, with the decision, the call or guarding of the question, this "piety" of thought.[4] This decision, this call or this guarding: is it already the question? Is it still the question? And why *almost* never? We must be patient here. I would have liked, then, to understand to what extent this privileging of questioning itself remained protected. Precisely *not* protected from a question, nor from a thought of the unthought coming down again to the Heideggerian determination of the un-thought (one single and unique thought for every *great* thinker, and therefore *one* un-thought, it simple too, which is only *un-gedacht* insofar as it is, in a non-negative way, un-*gedacht*,[5] so still a thought, as is marked by the intonation, the accentuation, the emphasis, these modes of avoidance or unavoidance which I was speaking of just now). Not, then, protected from a question, but from something else. Now *Geist,* as I will attempt to show, is perhaps the name Heidegger gives, beyond any other name, to this unquestioned possibility of the question.

A second thread conducts, especially in the great question of technology, to this typical and exemplary statement: the essence of technology is nothing technological. This matrix statement remains, at least in one of its aspects, traditionally philosophical. It maintains the possibility of thought that questions, which is always thought of the essence, protected from any original and essential contamination by technology. The concern, then, was to analyze this desire for rigorous non-contamination and, from that, perhaps, to envisage the necessity, one could say the fatal necessity of a *contamination*—and the word was important to me—of a contact originarily impurifying thought or speech by technology. Contamination, then, of the thought of essence by technology, and so contamination by technology of the thinkable essence of technology—and even of a question of technology by technology, the privilege of the question having some relation already, always, with this irreducibility of technology. It is easy to imagine that the consequences of this necessity cannot be limited. Yet *Geist,* as I will try to suggest, also names what Heidegger wants to save from any destitution (*Entmachtung*). It is even perhaps, beyond what must be saved, the very thing that saves (*rettet*). But what saves would not let itself be saved from this contamination. What happens here will be in the difference between *Geistigkeit* and a certain (non-Christian) *Geist- lichkeit* of the *Geist* whose purity Heidegger wants to save, a purity internal to spirit, even though he recognizes that evil (*das Böse*) is spiritual (*geistlich*).

The third thread leads back to what remains for me a very old anxiety, a still lively suspicion, whether in relation to Heidegger or to others. It concerns the discourse of animality and the axiomatic, explicit or not, which controls it. I have made numerous references to this, over a very long period.[6] Three years ago, during the work on *Geschlecht*, and in a lecture which some of you will know,[7] I offered a long analysis of Heidegger's discourse on the hand, wherever this discourse takes shape—be it a thematic occurrence, as in a passage of *Was heisst Denken?* (monkeys have prehensile organs, but only man "has" the hand; or, rather, the hand— and not the hands—holds the essence of man) or be it, ten years earlier, the seminar on Parmenides which takes up again the meditation around *pragma, praxis, pragmata*. These last present themselves as *vorhandene* or *zuhandene*, and so in the domain of the hand (*im Bereich der Hand*).[8] This problem concerns once more the relationship between animals and technology. This occurs in particular by means of a very problematical opposition, it seems to me, between *giving* and *taking*. It organizes this passage of *Was heisst Denken?*; it dictates the relations between prehension and reason (*vernehmen, Vernunft*), the relations between speech and the hand, the essence of writing as handwriting (*Handschrift*) outside of any technical mechanization or writing machine. The interpretation of the hand, like the opposition between human and animal *Dasein*, dominates in a thematic or nonthematic way Heidegger's most continuous discourse, from the repetition of the question of the meaning of Being, the destruction of onto-theology, and, first of all, from the existential analytic which redistributes the limits between *Dasein, Vorhandensein*, and *Zuhandensein*. Every time it is a question of hand and animal—but these themes cannot be circumscribed—Heidegger's discourse seems to me to fall into a rhetoric which is all the more peremptory and authoritarian for having to hide a discomfiture. In these cases it leaves intact, sheltered in obscurity, the axioms of the profoundest metaphysical humanism: and I do mean the profoundest. This is particularly manifest in the *Fundamental Concepts of Metaphysics*,[9] around some guiding theses to which I shall return later: the stone is without world (*weltlos*), the animal is poor in world (*weltarm*), man is world-forming (*weltbildend*). I tried to bring out the implications of these theses, their aporetical and nondissimulated difficulty or their interminably preparatory character. Why does Heidegger present such propositions as "theses," which is something he practically never does elsewhere, and for essential reasons? Do not these "theses" affect in turn all the concepts used in them, beginning with those of life and world? One can already see that these difficulties communicate with that of the *Fragen* (the animal isn't really capable of it), with that of technology, and finally, again, with that of spirit: what of the relationship between spirit and humanity, spirit and life, spirit and animality?

The fourth thread, finally, leads, through the thinking of *epochality*, in itself and in the way it is put to work, into what I shall call, a little provocatively, the hidden teleology or the narrative order. I insisted on the examples of the *chora*, of the foreclosure of certain bodies of thought, such as that of Spinoza on the principle of sufficient reason, etc. But once again, we shall see that epochal discrimination can be ordered around the difference—let us call it intraspiritual difference—between the Platonic-Christian, metaphysical or onto-theological determination of the spiritual (*geistig*), and another thinking of the spiritual as spoken, for example, in the *Gespräch* with Trakl: this time it is the *geistliche*, now withdrawn, as Heidegger *would like*, from its Christian or ecclesial signification.

That, then, is just about the point I had reached when I decided to speak of spirit. I shall do so with a negative certainty and a hypothesis: the certainty of not fully understanding what, in the end, rules Heidegger's *spiritual* idiom, and the hypothesis that more clarity, perhaps the ambiguous clarity of flame, would bring us nearer to the nexus of some unthoughts, to the interlacing of these four threads.

Needless to say, these unthoughts may well be mine and mine alone. And what would be more serious, more drily serious, they may well *give* nothing. "The more original a thought," says Heidegger, "the richer its Un-thought becomes. The Unthought is the highest gift (*Geschenk*) that a thought can give."[10]

III

To my knowledge, Heidegger never asked himself "What is spirit?" At least, he never did so in the mode, or in the form, or with the developments that he grants to questions such as: "Why is there something rather than nothing?" "What is Being?" "What is technology?" "What is called thinking?" etc. No more did he make of spirit one of those grand poles that metaphysics is supposed to have opposed to Being, in a sort of limitation (*Beschränkung*) of Being, such as is contested by the *Introduction to Metaphysics:* Being and becoming, Being and appearance, Being and thinking, Being and duty, or Being and value. No more did he oppose spirit to nature, even dialectically, according to the most forceful and permanent of metaphysical demands.

What is called spirit? What does spirit call up? *Was heisst der Geist?*—the title of a book Heidegger never wrote. When they have to do with spirit, Heidegger's statements *rarely* take the form of a definition of essence. Rarely, that is to say exceptionally, and we are interested in these exceptions which are in fact very different, and even opposed to each other. Most often, Heidegger will have *inscribed* the noun (*Geist*) or the adjective (*geistig, geistlich*): say in a linked group of concepts or philosophemes belonging to a deconstructible ontology, and most often in a sequence going from Descartes to Hegel, in other words in propositions which I will again risk calling axiomatic, axiological, or axio-poetic: the spiritual, then, no longer belongs to the order of these metaphysical or onto-theological meanings. Rather than a value, spirit seems to designate, beyond a deconstruction, the very resource for any deconstruction and the possibility of any evaluation. What then does he call spirit, *Geist*? In *Sein und Zeit*, it is first of all a word whose meaning remains steeped in a sort of ontological obscurity. Heidegger recalls this and asks for the greatest possible vigilance on this point. The word relates back to a series of meanings which have a common feature: to be opposed to the thing, to the metaphysical determination of thing-ness, and above all to the thingification of the subject, of the subjectivity of the subject as supposed by Descartes. This is the series of soul, consciousness, spirit, person. Spirit is not the thing, spirit is not the body. Of course, it is from this *subjective* determination of spirit that a delimitation (*Abgrenzung*) must disengage, one could say liberate, the existential analytic of *Dasein*. *Dasein* finds itself given the task of preparing a philosophical treatise on the question "What is man?" It should be remembered that it *precedes* (*liegt vor*, Heidegger's emphasis) all biology, all anthropology, all psychology. One could say all *pneumatology*, this being the other name Hegel gives to *rational psychology* which, further, he also criticizes as an "abstract metaphysics of understanding."[1]

The existential analytic has in particular to mark its distance from two attempts, two temptations also, and thus avoid the risk of seeing a genealogy where there is rather a leap, a rupture, at any rate a radical problematization.

On the one hand, one would get confused—this would be *irreführend*—if one thought of the Cartesian *cogito* as the right historical example, the exemplary precedent which opens the way to the existential analytic. This poses the ontological question of the *sum* which Descartes apparently left completely out of the question or out of the way [*hors lieu* (*völlig unerörtet*) (§10, p. 46)]. It would have been necessary to determine the Being of *sum* in order then to define the mode of Being of one's *cogitationes*. In starting, like

Descartes, from an *ego* and subject given immediately, one misses the phenomenality of *Dasein* (ibid.). The accusation is aimed also at the phenomenology of spirit and, in silence, at transcendental phenomenology and Husserl's *cogito*. Until it has been submitted to an ontological clarification, the idea of the subject continues to be bound up with the *positing* (*Ansatz*) of a *subjectum* or a *hypokeimenon*, and therefore of some substance or substratum, even if, at the purely ontic level, one is opposed to what could be called "*Seelensubstanz*," to psychic substantialism, or to any reification of consciousness (*Verdinglichung des Bewusstseins*) (ibid.). For in order to reject thingification or substantialization—a common gesture at the time of *Sein und Zeit*—one must also clarify the ontological provenance of what one understands by "thing," reality, or thing-ness (*Dinglichkeit*). If one does not clarify the ontological provenance of thing-ness, and a fortiori of substantiality, everything one understands "positively" (*positiv*) when one speaks of non-thingified Being (*dem nichtverdinglichten Sein*) of subject, soul, consciousness, spirit, person, etc., will remain ontologically problematic. Heidegger had already added to this series the *I* and reason. It goes without saying that the unconscious belongs to the same set. This was earlier on, in §6, entitled "The task of a deconstruction (*Destruktion*) of the history of ontology" (especially p. 22).

   Geist thus forms part of the series of non-things, of what in general one claims to oppose to the thing. It is what in no way allows itself to be thingified. But so long as the Being of what one understands by thing is not ontologically clarified—not done, apparently, by Descartes or Husserl, or by anyone who might have recommended us not to thingify the subject, soul, consciousness, spirit, person—these concepts remain problematic or dogmatic. At least they remain so from the point of view of an existential analytic of *Dasein*. All these words, and thus the word spirit, can, certainly, designate domains of phenomenality which a phenomenology could explore. But one can use them in this way only if one makes oneself indifferent to all questions about the Being of each of these entities.

These terms and these concepts have thus no rights in an analytic of *Dasein* which seeks to determine the entity which we ourselves are. Heidegger announces, then, that he is going to avoid them (*vermeiden*). In order to say what we are, who we are, it appears to be indispensable to *avoid* all the concepts in the subjective or *subjectal* series: in particular that of spirit (§10, p. 46).

Now who are we? Here, let us not forget, we are first and only determined from the opening to the *question of Being*. Even if Being must be given to us for that to be the case, we are only at this point, and know of "us" only this: the power or rather the possibility of questioning, the experience of questioning.

We were speaking a moment ago of the question. Now precisely this entity which we are, this "we" which, at the beginning of the existential analytic, must have no name other than *Da-sein*, is chosen for the position of exemplary entity only from *the experience of the question*, the possibility of the *Fragen*, as it is inscribed in the network of the *Gefragte* (Being), the *Erfragte* (the meaning of Being), of the *Befragte der Seinsfrage*, that is the entity which we are and which thus becomes the exemplary or privileged entity for a *reading*—Heidegger's word—of the meaning of Being. The point of departure in the existential analytic is legitimated first of all and only from the possibility, experience, structure, and regulated modifications of the *Fragen*. Such is the exemplarity of the entity which *we* are, of the *ourselves* in this discursive situation of *Mitsein* in which we can, to ourselves and to others, say *we*. This exemplarity can become or remain problematical. But this ought not to dissimulate a still less apparent problematicity—which is, precisely, perhaps no longer even a *problematicity*. It could not even be determined as question or problem. For it depends on this point of departure in a reflection on the question (it is better to say the *Fragen*) and its structural components. How, without confirming it a priori and circularly, can we *question* this inscription in the structure of the *Fragen* from which *Dasein* will have received, along with its privilege (*Vorrang*), its first, minimal, and most secure determination? Even supposing that this structure is described properly by Heidegger (which is not certain, but I leave that to one side for the moment), any worry as to the legitimacy or axiomatic necessity of such a point of departure in a reflection on the being-able-to-question would leave intact neither the principle, nor the order, nor finally the interest of the existential analytic: in three words, of *Sein und Zeit*. One would then turn against it what Heidegger says himself: however provisional the analysis, it always and already demands the assurance of a correct point of departure (§9, p. 43).

I insist on this point of departure in the possibility of the *Fragen* not only for the reasons I pointed out at the start. A few years later, when the references to spirit are no longer held in the discourse of *Destruktion* and in the analytic of *Dasein*, when the words *Geist* and *geistig* are no longer avoided, but rather *celebrated*, spirit itself will be defined by this manifestation and this force of the question. Of the question, then, *in the name of which* the same words are avoided in *Sein und Zeit*. When he says he must avoid them, Heidegger is right to emphasize that he does so not out of caprice, stubbornness, or concern for terminological oddness (§10, p. 46). The terms of this series: spirit, but also soul or *psyché*, consciousness, *ego*, reason, subject—and Heidegger adds on life and man too—block any interrogation on the Being of *Dasein*. They are all linked, as the unconscious would be just as well, to the Cartesian position of the *subjectum*. And even when they inspire the modernity of eloquent discourses on the non-thingification or non-reification of the subject, they—and in particular the terms life and man—mark a lack of interest, an indifference, a remarkable "lack of need" (*Bedürfnislosigkeit*) for the question of the Being of the entity which we are.

Each time one comes across the word "spirit" in this context and in this series, one should thus, according to Heidegger, recognize in it the same indifference: not only for the question of Being in general but for that of the entity which we are, more precisely for this *Jemeinigkeit*, this being-always-mine of *Dasein* which does not in the first place refer to a *me* or an ego and which had justified a first—prudent and, in the end, negative—reference to Descartes. The being-mine makes of *Dasein* something quite other than a case or an example of the genus of Being as *Vorhandene*. For what characterizes *Vorhandensein*? Well, precisely, the fact of being indifferent to its proper Being, to what it properly is. This indifference distinguishes it from *Dasein* which, for its part, has care for its Being. In truth, to the entity as *Vorhandene*, its Being is not even indifferent (*gleichgültig*). You cannot say that a stone is indifferent to its Being without being anthropomorphic. It is neither indifferent nor not indifferent (*weder gleichgültig noch ungleichgültig*). Heidegger does not wonder at this point (§9), and according to these categories, about animals. He would doubtless have some difficulties in doing so, but we will come back to this. On the other hand, it makes sense to say of *Dasein* that it can be indifferent to the question of its Being, precisely because it is not, because it *can*, also, *not be*. Its indifference in this case is only a modalization of its non-indifference. For *Dasein*, whose Being-mine can only pass into discourse by appealing to personal pronouns (*I am, you are*), indifference (*Indifferenz* this time, not *Gleichgültigkeit*) is one more way of relating itself to, interesting itself in, its proper Being, of not being indifferent to it. This last indifference (*Indifferenz*) to its own Being is not at all that of the stone or the table. It characterizes the everyday nature of *Dasein*, what in everydayness brings everything down to the average, this *Durchschnittlichkeit* which Heidegger claims he does not want to denounce as a negative phenomenon. Indifference in this case "is not nothing," but a "positive phenomenal characteristic."

Here then are *three types of indifference*. First, there is the absolute indifference of the *vorhandene* entity: the stone is placed even before the difference between indifference and its opposite. Second, there is indifference (*Indifferenz*) as a positive phenomenon of *Dasein*. There is further, *third*, the indifference which in the history of metaphysics, for example since Descartes, manifests this remarkable *Bedürfnislosigkeit nach dem Sein . . . zu fragen*, this lack of the need to ask questions about Being. And first of all about one's proper Being, about the Being of the entity which we are. This last indifference has a paralyzing effect as much when facing the thought of the thing-ness of the thing (*res, substantia*) as the thought of the subject (*hypokeimenon*). Through this indifference we keep to concepts such as spirit, soul, consciousness, person, etc. But there is an analogy between these two last manifestations of indifference, even a common condition of possibility. They lead of necessity to the limitation of the question of Being, to interpreting the "who" of *Dasein* as something which endures in a substantial identity of the type *Vorhandensein* or of the subject as *Vorhandensein*. As a result, however much one protests against the substantiality of the soul, the reification of consciousness, or the objectivity of the person, one continues to determine the "who" ontologically as a subject existing in the form of *Vorhandenheit*. The "spirit" granted it in that case is itself affected by this substantial subjectivity and this *Vorhandenheit*. Now what is the root of this interpretation that makes of the "who" an enduring form of existence? It is a vulgar concept of time. The concept of spirit must therefore be *avoided* insofar as it is itself founded on such an interpretation of time. Heidegger submits it to *Destruktion* in the course of this de-limitation (*Umgrenzung*) of the analytic of being-there. To say that the essence of being-there is "existence" in the sense Heidegger gives it then, is also to say that "the 'substance' of man is not spirit as a synthesis of the soul and the body but *existence*" (§25, p. 117). Let us note in passing that this concept of indifference does not provide any means of placing the animal. The animal, as Heidegger recognizes elsewhere, is certainly not a *Vorhandene*. So it does not have the absolute indifference of the stone, but no more does it have any share in the questioning "we," the starting point of the analysis of *Dasein*. It is not *Dasein*. Is it indifferent or not indifferent and in what sense? We will come back to this.

Descartes, then, did not displace medieval theology. In stopping at the distinction between *ens creatum* and *ens infinitum* or *increatum*, medieval theology failed to interrogate the Being of this *ens*. What passes for the rebirth or modern period of philosophical thinking is only the "rootedness of a deathly prejudice" which held back an ontological and thematic analytics of *Gemüt* (§6, p. 95). On the horizon, if not on the program of all this deconstruction (*Destruktion*) of spirit, there appears to be assigned a task, the destiny or further becoming of which in Heidegger's work ought to be followed: the "thematic ontological analytic of *Gemüt*." Is there a French equivalent for this last word? A word for word? I don't see one. If one day *Sein und Zeit* were to be translated [into French], I do not know which term would be the least inadequate. Boehm and de Waelhens well understood that it was necessary to avoid all the French words which might tempt the translator and immediately throw him off the track: *esprit* [spirit], *âme* [soul], *cœur* [heart]. They then imagined a strange stratagem, a foreign recourse: take up the Latin and Cartesian word *mens*, which not only does not *translate* but reintroduces into the program the very thing that had to be avoided. At least the artificial detour via *mens* signals a difficulty. It escapes the worst confusion. What would be the worst confusion? Well, the translation of *Gemüt* by "esprit," precisely at the very moment when Heidegger prescribes, in this very context, that one avoid (*vermeiden*) this word. Now this is the very word towards which the Martineau-Vezin translation (Paris: Gallimard, 1985) rushes headlong, as if to confuse everything.

The same de-limitation affects just as much the "sciences of spirit," history as science of spirit or psychology as science of spirit (*geisteswissenschaftliche Psychologie*), and all the conceptual apparatus organized around *psyché* and life in Dilthey, Bergson, in personalisms or philosophical anthropologies. Heidegger allows for the differences between these, but he inscribes in the same set all those who refer to life and intentional structure. Whether in Husserl or Scheler, it is the same inability to interrogate the Being of the person. Comparable developments are to be found in *The Fundamental Problems of Phenomenology* (§15). In short, at this point, the concept of spirit, *this* concept of spirit must be deconstructed. What it lacks, apart from any ontological question as to what makes man a unity (soul, consciousness, spirit *and* body), is thus indeed an analytic of *Gemüt*.

IV

Should we close *Sein und Zeit* at this point? Do the many developments devoted to the heritage of the Cartesian graft add nothing to these premises? Is this the book's last word on the theme of spirit?

Yes and no.

Yes, insofar as the premises and the deconstruction will *never* be called into question again. Neither in *Sein und Zeit* nor later.

No, because the rhetorical strategy is displaced when a step is taken, already, in the direction of this analytic of *Gemüt*. As early as *Sein und Zeit*, Heidegger takes up the values and the word "spirit," simply *in quotation marks*. He thus assumes it without assuming it, he avoids it in no longer avoiding it. To be sure, this un-avoidance now supposes and will henceforth maintain the earlier delimitation. It does not contradict, but confirms and renews the necessity of avoiding (*vermeiden*), and will always do so. And yet, along with the word, even enclosed in quotation marks, something of spirit—doubtless what signals towards *Gemüt*—allows itself to be withdrawn from the Cartesian-Hegelian metaphysics of subjectivity. Something which the word "spirit" still names between quotation marks thus allows itself to be salvaged. Spirit returns. The word "spirit" starts to become acceptable again. The catharsis of the quotation marks frees it from its vulgar, *uneigentlich*, in a word Latino-Cartesian, marks. There then begins, at the other end of the same book, the slow work of reappropriation which will merge, as I should like to demonstrate, with a re-Germanization.

This time it has to do with space and time.

As for space, first of all, Heidegger begins (*this is only a first move*) by avoiding, purely and simply, the traditional concept of spirit. *Dasein* is not a *spiritual* interiority, the secondary nature of which would have to be derived from a becoming-spatial. It has its own being-in-space (*ein eigenes "im-Raum-sein"*). But this latter is possible only on the basis of its being-in-the-world in general. One must not say that being-in-a-world (*das In-Sein in einer Welt*) is a spiritual property (*eine geistige Eigenschaft*). One must not say that man's spatiality characterizes his body alone. If one did say this, one would return to the obscure problem of a being-together, in the form of *Vorhandensein* of a bodily thing (*Körperding*) and a spiritual thing (*Geistding*). The obscurity of the thing would remain entire. One would be giving in to the naive opinion (*naïve Meinung*) according to which a man, a spiritual thing, would see himself *after the fact* (*nachträglich*) transposed, transferred, deported (*versetzt*) into a space (§12, p. 56).

But in a *second move*, the same logic this time imposes recourse to quotation marks. The word "spirit" returns, it is no longer rejected, avoided, but used in its deconstructed sense to designate something other which resembles it, and of which it is, as it were, the metaphysical ghost, the spirit of another spirit. Between the quotation marks, through the grid they impose, one sees a double of spirit announcing itself. More precisely, spirit visible in its letter, scarcely legible, becomes as it were the spectral silhouette—but already legible, this one—of another. The spectrality would be no more an accident of spirit than of *Geist*, of the thing and of the word. Through the word of Cartesian metaphysics or of the subjective graft, traversing it like an index finger showing something beyond itself, Heidegger will name, in quotation marks, in other words will *write*—negatively, indirectly, silently—something which is not, to be sure, what the old discourse called "spirit," but *in any case, above all, not* what it would have considered as *the opposite of spirit: the spatial thing, the outside, the body, the inanimate,* etc. What is at stake now is to stress that spatiality does not *befall* a spiritual *Dasein* which would, through the body, fall after the fact into space. To the contrary, it is because *Dasein* is not a *vorhandene* thing that it is spatial, but quite differently spatial from what one calls physical and extended things. It is thus *because* it is "spiritual" (this time in quotation marks, of course) that it is spatial and that its spatiality remains original. It is by virtue of this "spirituality" that *Dasein* is a being of space and, Heidegger even underlines it, *only by virtue* of such a "spirituality." We must make ourselves attentive in the first instance to these mute signs—the quotation marks and the underlining:

> Neither can the spatiality of *Dasein* be interpreted as an imperfection which would be inherent to existence by virtue of the fatal "union of spirit with a body." *Dasein* can, to the contrary, because it is "spiritual" (*"geistig"*), and *only for that reason* (*und nur deshalb*) be spatial according to a modality which remains essentially impossible for an extended corporeal thing. (§70, p.368)

Further on in the book, the quotation marks provide the same surveillance around the word "spirit" when it is no longer a question of space, on this occasion, but of time. However, despite the analogous logical or rhetorical movement, what is at stake is not symmetrical. The development now belongs to a veritable thematics of spirit, and more precisely of the Hegelian interpretation of the relations between spirit and time (§82). If, as Hegel says, "history, which is essentially history of spirit, unfolds 'in time'," if therefore "the development of history falls (*fällt*) into time," how can spirit thus fall into time, into this pure sensible order, this "insensible sensible" (*das unsinnliche Sinnliche*)? For such a fall to be possible, the essence of time and the essence of spirit must have been interpreted in a certain fashion by Hegel. Heidegger says that he does not with to criticize (*kritisieren*) this double interpretation, treat it as though it were simply not to his taste. The argumentation now becomes tortuous and would merit a long analysis. What has to be brought out? That the idea of a fall of spirit into time presupposes a vulgar concept of time. It is "against" (*gegen*) this Hegelian concept of time, against this vulgar concept, *with it as backdrop*, that authentic, proper, nonvulgar temporality stands out, the temporality which forms the transcendental horizon of the question of Being in *Sein und Zeit*. For the Hegelian concept of time represents or presents (*darstellt*)—Heidegger says this has not been sufficiently noticed—"the most radical conceptual elaboration of the vulgar understanding of time" (§82, p.428).

If spirit "falls" into a time itself determined as negation of the negation, it must also present *itself* as negation of the negation. Its essence is the concept, i.e., the form of thought when it thinks itself, the *self*-conceiving (*das* sich *Begreifen*) *as grasping* of the non-I (als Erfassen *des Nicht-Ich*), in other words a grasping of this difference. There is thus in the pure concept, the essence of spirit, a difference of difference (*ein Unterscheiden des Unterschieds*). It is just this which gives the essence of spirit the formal apophantic determination which was required—that of a negation of the negation. And it is indeed a logical formalization of the Cartesian *cogito*, i.e. of consciousness as *cogito me cogitare rem*, grasping of self as grasping of non-self. The Hegelian determination of spirit indeed remains ordered, prescribed, ruled by the epoch of the Cartesian *cogito*. It therefore calls for the same deconstruction. Did not Hegel hail Descartes as the Christopher Columbus of philosophical modernity?

If there is an identity of formal structure between spirit and time, i.e., the negation of the negation, it remains to be explained that one of them appears to "fall" into the other. In their formal abstraction, spirit and time are outside, exteriorized, divested (*entäussert*), whence their affinity (*Verwandschaft*). But Hegel always conceives of time in vulgar fashion, as "levelled world-time" the provenance of which remains hidden. He still interprets time as a *Vorhandenes*, an entity standing there in front, facing spirit, itself understood in the sense of subjectity. Time, the being-there of the concept, and so the being-there of the essence of spirit, is *there in front*, facing spirit, outside it and as its opposite (*steht sie dem Geist als ein Vorhandenes einfach gegenüber*). One must be coming from this vulgar interpretation to say of spirit that it "falls into time," *into* a time which is there *in front* of it, as though external to it, opposed (*gegenüber*), present after the fashion of an ob-ject. But what is signified by this fall and this effectuation (*Verwirklichung*) of spirit into a time which remains foreign or external to it, even though it has power over it? According to Heidegger, Hegel says nothing about this, he leaves it obscure. No more does he ask the question as to whether the essential constitution of spirit *as* negation of negation is not in fact possible only on the basis of an originary and non-vulgar temporalization.

Now it is precisely when he undertakes to explicate this originary temporality that Heidegger finally takes up the word "spirit" as his own, and twice, but *twice in quotation marks*. We were saying just now that these quotation marks, although analogous, were not simply symmetrical to those enclosing the word "*geistig*" in the analysis of the spatiality of *Dasein*. This is due to the obvious privileging of time. According to the declared project of *Sein und Zeit*, we know that time forms the transcendental horizon of existential analysis, of the question of the meaning of Being and of any related question in this context.

Two sentences, then, and twice *"Der 'Geist'"* in quotation marks.

This is the first sentence at the end of the same paragraph 82:

"Spirit" does not first fall into time, but it *exists* (*existiert*, italicized) as originary *temporalization* (*Zeitigung*, italicized) of temporality. This temporalizes the time of the world in the horizon of which "history" [also in quotation marks, I emphasize the fact, JD] as intratemporal happening can appear.

At this point, still playing with the quotation marks, Heidegger will displace the fall. *Fallen* will no longer be the *Fallen* of spirit into time, but the lowering, the descent, or the degradation of an original temporalization into a temporality that is separated into different levels, inauthentic, improper, such as it is represented by the vulgar interpretation of Cartesian-Hegelianism: as a *Vorhandenes*. There is indeed, in quotation marks, a "spirit," but it does not fall into time. There is indeed a "fall," in quotation marks, but the falls it causes are from one time to the other, I dare not say from time to time or now and then [*de temps en temps ou de temps à autre*]. The falls it causes are not *from spirit* [*de l'esprit*] into time. But from time into time, one time into another. And if "spirit" in quotation marks becomes temporalization itself, one ought just as much to speak of the fall of one spirit into the other. In the sentence I am about to read, the "*Fallen*" in quotation marks (citing Hegel) relates back to *Verfallen* as it is written without quotation marks in the analytic of *Dasein:*

"Spirit" (*Der "Geist"*) does not fall *into* time, but: factitious existence (*die faktische Existenz*) "falls" ("*fällt*") in that it falls (*als verfallende*) *from* (or outside, *aus*, italicized) originary and proper temporality (authentic: *ursprüngliche, eigentliche Zeitlichkeit*). But this "falling" itself has its existential possibility in a mode of its temporalization which belongs to temporality. [§82, p. 436]

In a word, in two words, in a word or two, spirit does not fall into time, as Hegel says. In another sense and with the obligatory quotation marks, spirit is essentially temporalization. If fall there be, as Heidegger also thinks, it is for reasons that are essential, that form for *Sein und Zeit* the very horizon of the question of Being: there is a falling from one time into the other. It is neither evil nor accident, it is not an accidental evil. But we already perceive, behind or between the quotation marks, this spirit which is not other than time. It returns, in short, to time, to the movement of temporalization, it lets itself be affected in itself, and not accidentally, as from outside, by something like falling or *Verfallen*. We will have to remind ourselves of this much later when Heidegger insists on the spiritual essence of evil. But the focus then will be on *Geistlichkeit* and no longer on *Geistigkeit*. This spirituality will determine a semantic value for the word *geistlich*, which Heidegger will even want to de-Christianize, although it belongs in common parlance to the church code. There is thus a vast distance to cover.

We are still in 1926–27. Despite its discreet turbulence, despite this doubling which seems already to affect it with an obsessive specter, Heidegger does not take up as his own the word "spirit"; he barely gives it shelter. At any rate, the hospitality offered is not without reservation. Even when it is admitted, the word is contained at the doorstep or held at the frontier, flanked with discriminatory signs, held at a distance by the procedure of quotation marks. Through these artifices of writing it is, to be sure, the same word, but also another. In order to describe this situation, let us momentarily, for convenience, provisionally resort to the distinction put forward by speech-act theory between *use* and *mention*. It would not be to Heidegger's taste, but perhaps what is at stake is also to put the limits of such a distinction to the test. Heidegger began by *using* the word "spirit." More precisely, he first of all *used* it *negatively*, he mentioned it as the word no longer to use. He *mentioned* its possible *use* as what had to be excluded. Then, in a second moment, he used it on his own account but with quotation marks, as though still mentioning the discourse of the other, as though citing or borrowing a word he wanted to put to another use. What counts most is the sentence in which this subtle—in fact inextricable—interlacing of "use" and "mention" is done. The sentence transforms and displaces the concept. With its quotation marks, as with the discursive context which determines them, it calls for another word, another appellation, unless it alter the same word, the same appellation, unless it re-call the other under the same.

V

It's the law of quotation marks. Two by two they stand guard: at the frontier or before the door, assigned to the threshold in any case, and these places are always dramatic. The apparatus lends itself to theatricalization, and also to the hallucination of the stage and its machinery: two pairs of pegs hold in suspension a sort of drape, a veil or a curtain. Not closed, just slightly open. There is the time this suspension lasts: six years, the suspense of the spectator and the tension which follows the credits. Then, suddenly, with a single blow and not three, the lifting [*levée*] of the quotation marks marks the raising [*lever*] of the curtain. And there's a *coup de théâtre* immediately, with the overture: the entry on stage of spirit itself, unless it's delegating its ghost, its *Geist*, again.

Six years later, 1933, and here we have the *Rectorship Address:* the curtain-raising is also the spectacle of academic solemnity, the splendor of the staging celebrating the quotation marks' disappearance. In the wings, spirit was waiting for its moment. And here it makes its appearance. It presents itself. Spirit *itself*, spirit in its spirit and in its letter, *Geist* affirms itself through the self-affirmation of the German university. Spirit's affirmation, inflamed. Yes, *inflamed:* I say this not only to evoke the pathos of the *Rectorship Address* when it celebrates spirit, not only because of what a reference to flame can illuminate of the terrifying moment which is deploying its specters around this theater, but because twenty years later, exactly twenty years, Heidegger

31

will say of *Geist*, without which it is impossible to think Evil, that *in the first place* it is neither *pneuma* nor *spiritus*, thus allowing us to conclude that *Geist* is no more heard in the Greece of the philosophers than in the Greece of the Gospels, to say nothing of Roman deafness: *Geist* is flame. And this could, apparently, be said, and thus thought, only in German.

How are we to explain this sudden inflammation and inflation of *Geist*? *Sein und Zeit* was all tortuous prudence, the severe economy of a writing holding back declaration within a discipline of severely observed markers. So how does Heidegger get from this to the eloquent fervor and the sometimes rather righteous proclamation dedicated to the self-affirmation of the German university? What is the leap from the one to the other? And what in spite of this is confirmed and continued from the one to the other?

Each word of the title, *die Selbstbehauptung der deutschen Universität*, is traversed, steeped, illuminated, determined (*bestimmt*)—I mean both defined and destined—called for, by spirit. Self-affirmation, first of all, would be impossible, would not be heard, would not be what it is if it were not of the order of spirit, spirit's very order. The word "order" designating both the value of command, of leading, duction or conduction, the *Führung*, and the value of mission: sending, an order given. Self-affirmation *wants* to be (we must emphasize this wanting) the affirmation of spirit through *Führung*. This is a spiritual conducting, of course, but the *Führer*, the guide—here the Rector—says he can only lead if he is himself led by the inflexibility of an order, the rigor or even the *directive* rigidity of a mission (*Auftrag*). This is also, already, spiritual. Consequently, conducted from guide to guide, the self-affirmation of the German university will be possible only through those who lead, while themselves being led, directors directed by the affirmation of this spiritual mission. Later, we shall have to recognize a passage between this *affirmation* and a certain thinking of consent, of commitment in the form of a reply, of a responsible acquiescence, of agreement or confidence (*Zusage*), a sort of word given in return. Before any question and to make possible the question itself.

The *German* character of this university is not a secondary or contingent predicate, it cannot be dissociated from this affirmation of spirit. As the highest agency of the institution thus erected, of this "high school" (*hohe Schule*), directed upwards from the heights, spirit can do nothing other than affirm itself—and this, as we shall hear, in the movement of an authentication or identification which *wish themselves to be properly German*.

Right from the opening of the *Address*, Heidegger himself emphasizes the adjective "spiritual" (*geistig*). It is thus the first thing he stresses. I shall emphasize it in my turn, reading Gérard Granel's [French] translation: not only because it is the first word to be stressed, but because this adjective, *geistig*, is the word which twenty years later will be opposed to *geistlich*. The latter would no longer have anything Platonic-metaphysical or Christian-metaphysical about it, whereas *geistig*, Heidegger will say then, in his own name and not in a commentary on Trakl, remains caught in the metaphysico-Platonic-Christian oppositions of the below and the beyond, of the low and the high, of the sensible and the intelligible. And yet, in the *Rectorship Address*, the *Geistigkeit* to which Heidegger appeals is already opposed to "the Christo-theological interpretation of the world which followed" (*Die nachkommende christlich-theologische Weltdeutung*).[1] But there is no *Geistlichkeit* yet. Is this simply a terminological incoherence, a verbal adjustment which takes a certain time? Up to a point, without doubt, but I do not think that things can be reduced to that.

Here, then, is the first paragraph of the *Rectorship Address*, the lifting of the quotation marks, which are carried off, the raising of the curtain on the first act, the inaugural

celebration of spirit: cortege, academic procession—spirit is
at the head, and in the highest, since it leads the very lead-
ers. It precedes, anticipates [*prévient*] and gives the direction
to be followed—to the *spiritus rector* (whose directives we
know better today) and to those who follow him:

> To take over the rectorship is to oblige oneself to guide
> this high school *spiritually* (*die Verpflichtung zur* geis-
> tigen *Führung dieser hohen Schule*). Those who follow,
> masters and pupils, owe their existence and their
> strength only to a true common rootedness in the es-
> sence of the German university. But this essence
> comes to the clarity, the rank and the power which are
> its own only if first of all and at all times the guiders
> [*guideurs*] (*Führer:* I prefer "guide" to "guider," a rather
> rare and perhaps neologistic word, which runs the risk
> of making us forget that *Führer* was at that time very
> common in German) are themselves guided—guided
> by the inflexibility of this spiritual mission (*jenes geis-
> tige Auftrags*), the constraining nature of which im-
> prints the destiny of the German people with its spe-
> cific historical character. (p.5 [470])

This final sentence speaks, then, of the imprint (*Gepräge*)
marked in the destiny of the German people. A typological
motif, and even an onto-typological motif, as Lacoue-
Labarthe would put it. Its recurrences in the *Rectorship Address* must be interrogated retrospectively in light of the
letter to Jünger (*Zur Seinsfrage*) and what relates there to the
modern accomplishment of subjectity. Without being able to
enter into this problem, I would point out that the figure of
the imprint is associated here, regularly and essentially,
with that of force. Heidegger says sometimes *Prägekraft* (p.
5 [470]) or *prägende Kraft* (p. 20 [477]). Now force is just as
regularly, just as essentially, associated with spirit in the
sense that it is celebrated thereafter without quotation
marks.

At the centre of the *Address,* for the first time to my knowledge (subsequently he does so only twice, in texts on Schelling and on Trakl), Heidegger offers a definition of spirit. It is certainly presented in the form of a definition: S is P. And without any possible doubt, Heidegger takes it up for his own. He is no longer mentioning the discourse of the other. No longer speaking of spirit as in Descartes, Hegel, or later Schelling or Hölderlin, he links this predicative determination to a series of headings whose importance there is no need for me to stress. I will name *four* of them to prepare for the reading of this definition.

1. First there is *questioning, Fragen,* which manifests here—and manifests *itself*—as will: will to know and will to essence. Even before the definition of spirit, which reaffirms it, this will had been affirmed earlier in the *Address:*

To will the essence of the German university is to will science, in the sense of willing the spiritual historical mission of the German people (*Wille zum geschichtlichen geistegen Auftrag des deutschen Volkes*) as a people that knows itself in its State. Science and German destiny must, in this will to essence, achieve power (*Macht*) *at the same time.* (p.7 [471])

2. Next there is the *world,* a central theme of *Sein und Zeit.* Like the renewed quest of *Fragen,* it marks the profound continuity between *Sein und Zeit* and the *Address.*
3. Further, and still linked to force, there is the theme of *earth-and-blood:* "erd- und bluthaften Kräfte als Macht...."
4. Finally, and above all, still in essential and internal continuity with *Sein und Zeit,* there is *Entschlossenheit: resolution,* determination, the decision which gives its possibility of opening to *Eigentlichkeit,* the authentic property of *Dasein.*

Here now is this key paragraph, with these *four determinations of spirit:*

If we want the essence of science in the sense of *this manner of holding firm, questioning (fragenden) and exposed, in the midst of the uncertainty of entities in their totality,* then this will to essence creates for our people its most intimate and extreme world of danger, in other words its true *spiritual* world *(seine wahrhaft* geistige *Welt: geistige* is underlined). For "spirit" [in quotation marks, but this time to recall in a still negative definition the spirit others talk of] is neither empty sagacity, nor the gratuitous game of joking [*Spiel des Witzes:* this distinction between spirit and the *mot d'esprit,* ·between *Geist* and *Witz,* recalls the Kant of the *Anthropology* noting that a feature of the French spirit was marked in the fact that French has only one word, the word *esprit,* to designate *Witz* and *Geist*], nor the unlimited work of analysis of the understanding, nor even the reason of the world [probably an allusion to Hegel], but spirit is the being-resolved to the essence of Being *(ursprünglich gestimmte, wissende Entschlossenheit zum Wesen des Seins),* of a resolution which accords with the tone of the origin and which is knowledge [*savoir*]. And the *spiritual world (geistige Welt,* underlined) of a people is not the superstructure of a culture, and no more is it an arsenal of bits of knowledge [*connaissances*] and usable values, but the deepest power of conservation of its forces of earth and blood, as the most intimate power of e-motion *(macht der innersten Erregung)* and the vastest power of disturbance of its existence *(Dasein).* Only a spiritual world *(Eine geistige Welt allein)* guarantees the people its grandeur. For it imposes the constraint that the constant decision between the will to grandeur on the one hand, and on the other the *laisser-faire* of decadence *(des Verfalls),* give its rhythm to the

march our people has begun toward its future history.
(pp. 13–14 [474–75])

The celebration corresponds properly, literally, to an *exaltation* of the spiritual. It is an elevation. This is not only a question of the kerygmatic tone, of proclamation or declaration. But of an exaltation in which is declared and erected the most high. As always, the profound and the haughty are allied in the most high: the highest of what guides the spiritual guides of *die hohe Schule* and the depth of the forces of earth and blood. For it is, precisely, in them that the spiritual world consists. As to what is clear in this exaltation, spirit has here no longer the sense of metaphysical subjectity. There is no contradiction with *Sein und Zeit* in this regard. Spirit does not belong to subjectity, *at least* in its psychical or egological form, for it is not certain that the massive voluntarism of this *Address* is not still caught up in the same epoch of subjectity.

One other thing seems as clear: in a sense which would, to be sure, *like* to think itself not Hegelian, historicity is immediately and essentially determined as spiritual. And what is true of history is true of the world. On several occasions, Heidegger associates, with a hyphen, the adjectives *geistig* and *geschichtlich: geistig-geschichtlich* is *Dasein* (p. 17 [477]), *geschichtlich-geistig* is the world (p. 18 [477]). This association will be constant, two years later, in the *Introduction to Metaphysics*. But still in the *Address*, and still in order to follow this trace of the question and its privilege, I shall insist on the following point: the union, the hyphen [*trait d'union*] between spirit and history plays a very significant role in a passage which makes of the *Fragen* the very assignment of spirit. The question is *of spirit* or it is not:

Such an original concept of science carries the obligation not only of "objectivity" ("*Sachlichkeit*"), but again and above all of the essentiality and simplicity of questioning (*des Fragens*) at the center of the spiritual world which is, historially, that of the people (*inmitten der geschichtlich-geistigen Welt des Volkes*). And even, it is solely from this that objectivity can receive its true foundation, in other words find its genre and its limits. (ibid. [477])

The self-affirmation of the German university: every word of the title is, as we said, steeped in the exalting celebration of this spirit. We have just seen how the force of its imprint marks the self-affirmation, signing in the *same stroke* the being-German of the people and of their world, that is, its university as will to know and will to essence. It remains to confirm that the same spiritual imprint is inscribed in the academic organization, in the legislation of faculties and departments, in the community (*Gemeinschaft*) of masters and pupils:

The faculty is a faculty only if it deploys itself in a capacity for spiritual legislation (*geistiger Gesetzgebung*) rooted in the essence of science, so as to give to the powers of existence (*Mächte des Daseins*), which form its urgency, the form of the people's one spiritual world (*die eine geistige Welt des Volkes*) (ibid. [478])

As for what is commanded or recommended *of spirit* in it, this *Address* calls for *at least* three readings, three evaluations, or rather three protocols of interpretation.

1. To the extent that he countersigns the assignment of spirit, the author of this *Address*, as such, cannot exempt himself from any responsibility.

His discourse is first of all that of response and responsibility. Responsibility properly assumed, or even claimed before different authorities. These latter are always associated among themselves inasmuch as they are united with spirit. Spirit writes their hyphen, the hyphen between the world, history, the people, the will to essence, the will to know, the existence of *Dasein* in the experience of the question.

2. This responsibility is nonetheless exercised according

to a strategy. Tortuous, at least double, the strategy can always hold an extra surprise in reserve for whoever thinks he controls it.

On the one hand, Heidegger thus confers the most reassuring and elevated *spiritual* legitimacy on everything in which, and on all before whom, he commits himself, on everything he thus sanctions and consecrates at such a height. One could say that he spiritualizes National Socialism. And one could reproach him for this, as he will later reproach Nietzsche for having exalted the spirit of vengeance into a "spirit of vengeance spiritualized to the highest point" (*ein höchst vergeistigter Geist der Rache*).[2]

But, on the other hand, by taking the risk of spiritualizing nazism, he might have been trying to absolve or save it by marking it with this affirmation (spirituality, science, questioning, etc.). By the same token, this sets apart [*démarque*] Heidegger's commitment and breaks an affiliation. This address *seems* no longer to belong simply to the "ideological" camp in which one appeals to obscure forces—forces which would not be spiritual, but natural, biological, racial, according to an anything but spiritual interpretation of "earth and blood."

3. The force to which Heidegger appeals, and again in conclusion when he speaks of the destiny of the West, is thus a "spiritual force" (*geistige Kraft*). And we will find this theme of spirit and of the West again, though displaced, in the text on Trakl.

What is the price of this strategy? Why does it fatally turn back against its "subject"—if one can use this word, as one must, in fact? Because one cannot demarcate oneself from biologism, from naturalism, from racism in its genetic form, one cannot be *opposed* to them except by reinscribing spirit in an oppositional determination, by once again making it a unilaterality of subjectity, even if in its voluntarist form. The constraint of this program remains very strong, it reigns over the majority of discourses which, today and for a long time to come, state their opposition to racism, to totalitarianism, to nazism, to fascism, etc., and do this in the name of spirit, and even of the freedom of (the) spirit,[3] in the name of an axiomatic—for example, that of democracy or "human rights"—which, directly or not, comes back to this metaphysics of *subjectity*. All the pitfalls of the strategy of establishing demarcations belong to this program, whatever place one occupies in it. The only choice is the choice between the terrifying contaminations it assigns. Even if all forms of complicity are not equivalent, they are *irreducible*. The question of knowing which is the least grave of these forms of complicity is always there—its urgency and its seriousness could not be over-stressed—but it will never dissolve the irreducibility of this fact. This "fact" [*fait*], of course, is not simply a fact. First, and at least, because it is not yet *done* [*fait*], not altogether [*pas tout à fait*]: it calls more than ever, as for what in it remains to come after the disasters that have happened, for absolutely unprecedented responsibilities of "thought" and "action." This is what we should have to try to designate, if not to name, and begin to analyze here.

In the *Rectorship Address*, this risk is not just a risk run. If its program seems diabolical, it is because, *without there being anything fortuitous in this*, it capitalizes on the worst, that is on both evils at once: the sanctioning of nazism, and the gesture that is still metaphysical. Behind the ruse of quotation marks of which there is never the right amount (always too many or too few of them), this equivocation has to do with the fact that *Geist* is always haunted by its *Geist*: a spirit, or in other words, in French [and English] as in German, a phantom, always surprises by returning to be the other's ventriloquist. Metaphysics always returns, I mean in the sense of a *revenant* [ghost], and *Geist* is the most fatal figure of this *revenance* [returning, haunting]. Of the double which can never be separated from the single.

Is this not what Heidegger will never finally be able to

avoid (*vermeiden*), the unavoidable itself—spirit's double, *Geist* as the *Geist* of *Geist*, spirit as spirit of the spirit which always comes with its double? Spirit is its double. However we interpret this awesome equivocality, for Heidegger it is inscribed *in spirit*. It is *of spirit*. He will say so in speaking of spiritual evil in the text on Trakl. But he already notes it, in another mode, at the beginning of the *Introduction to Metaphysics*, two years after the *Rectorship Address*.

In the same way that, in spite of the *coup de théâtre*, the raising of the curtain or the lifting of the quotation marks, the *Address* relaunches and confirms the essential elements of *Sein und Zeit*, so the *Einführung* (1935) repeats the invocation of spirit launched in the *Address*. It even relaunches it, explains it, extends it, justifies it, specifies it, surrounds it with unprecedented precautions.

The rhetoric is no longer, to be sure, that of a treatise, as in *Sein und Zeit*, nor that of an inaugural and emphatic speech, as in the *Rekoratsrede*. Here we have a teaching language, which partakes of both genres simultaneously. No more than in 1933 does it rehabilitate the concept of spirit deconstructed in *Sein und Zeit*. But it is still in the name of spirit, the spirit which guides in resolution toward the question, the will to know and the will to essence, that the other spirit, its bad double, the phantom of subjectity, turns out to be warded off by means of *Destruktion*.

Is this duplicity the same as the equivocality or the ambiguity which Heidegger recalls right at the beginning of the *Introduction*, when he speaks of the *Zweideutigkeit* in which "every essential form of spirit" stands? [4] The more singular a figure of spirit, the more tempted one is to be mistaken about it, through comparison and confusion. Now philosophy is one of the essential forms of spirit: independent, creative, rare among the possibilities and the necessities of human *Dasein* in its historiality. Precisely because of its essential rarity, a singularity always inspires mistakes,

just as *Zweideutigkeit* inspires *Missdeutung*. The first misinterpretation consists in demanding first of all—we are still
very familiar with this program today—that philosophy procure for the *Dasein* and the age of a people the foundations
of a culture, and then denigrating philosophy when it is useless from this point of view and does not serve that culture.
Second expectation, second mistake: this figure of spirit,
philosophy, ought at the very least to procure system, syn-
opsis, world-picture (*Weltbild*), map of the world (*Welt-
karte*), a sort of compass for universal orientation. If philosophy cannot ground culture, then it should at least alleviate
and facilitate the technico-practical functioning of cultural
activities, and lighten the burden on science by taking off its
hands epistemological reflection on its presuppositions, its
concepts and its fundamental principles (*Grundbegriffe,
Grundsätze*). What is expected of the philosopher? That he
be the functionary of the fundamental. These misunder-
standings, more full of life today than ever, are sustained,
notes Heidegger (and who will argue with him?), by teachers
of philosophy.

Self-affirmation or self-presentation of spirit: all that the
Rectorship Address announces in these terms is renamed in
the *Einführung*. One could say from the title and name of
Einführung. The assignment of the question is here immediately associated with that of the *Führung* said to be *spiritual*. The *Einführung* opens with a meditation on the question, or more precisely on the *introduction to the question*,
on what introduces, induces, and conducts to within the
question, the *Hineinführen in das Fragen der Grundfrage*
(p.15 [21]).

There is no questioning except in the *experience* of the
question. Questions are not things, like water, stone, shoes,
clothes, or books. The *Hineinführen* into the question does
not conduct or induct *something*, it guides, conducts towards the experience, the awakening or the production of
the question. But as nothing ought to dictate the question,

nor precede it in its *freedom*, the *Führen* is *already* questioning. It comes before, it is an already questioning forecoming of the question (*ein fragendes Vorangehen*), a prequestioning, *ein Vor-fragen.* In this way, if nothing precedes the question in its freedom, not even the introduction to questioning, then the spirit of spiritual conduction (*geistige Führung*)—spoken of in both the *Rectorship Address* and the *Introduction to Metaphysics*—can be interpreted, through and through, as the possibility of questioning. It responds and corresponds to this possibility, unless this latter already responds or corresponds to it, in the ties and obligations or even the alliances of such a correspondence, as also in the experience of this co-responsibility. This discourse on spirit is also a discourse on the freedom of spirit.

Given that nothing precedes it, spiritual duction remains itself un-conducted, and thus breaks the circle of empty reflection which threatened the question of being in its fundamental form: "Why are there entities and not nothing?" That was the first sentence of the book. There was a risk that the reflexive machine would make it circle *ad infinitum* in the question of the question: why "why"? etc. Heidegger speaks rather of a leap (*Sprung*) of the question. The leap makes the originary upsurge (*Ursprung*) surge, liberates it without having to introduce the question from anything other than an *already* questioning conduction: *and this is spirit itself.* Spirit wakes, awakens rather [*plutôt*]—earlier [*plus tôt*]—from the *Vor-fragen* of the *Führung.* Nothing anticipates this power of awakening, in its freedom and its resolution (*Entschlossenheit*). What comes *before* and *in front,* what anticipates and questions before all else (*vor*), is spirit, the freedom of spirit. As *Führer,* it goes or comes on the way, in front, up in front, before all politics, all psychagogy, all pedagogy.

For in all honesty we must make clear the fact that at the very moment at which he runs the risk of placing this thematics of the *Führung* in the service of a determinate politics, Heidegger gives it to be understood that he is breaking in advance with any such service. In its spiritual essence, this free conducting must not give rise to any camp-following [*suivisme*], one should not accord it any following, any follower, any *Gefolgschaft*, any aggregation of disciples or partisans. One can naturally extend to the party what Heidegger says, to exclude them, of the School as academic study, technical apprenticeship, or professional training. Undoubtedly it will be difficult to understand what can be meant by a *Führung* which mandates, demands, or commands without being followed, obeyed, or listened to in any way. However spiritual it be, one will say, it must surely guide. Certainly, Heidegger would say here, but if one finds it difficult to understand, that means that one remains imprisoned in a logic of the understanding and does not accede to this freedom of listening, to this fidelity or modality of following which would have no relationship to the mindless following of *Gefolgschaft*. Perhaps. But it is also the case that, on the other hand, if it is not further reduced to its discursive modalities or to interrogative utterances, this questioning belongs through and through, that is to say essentially, to will and to will as the will to know. *"Fragen ist Wissen-wollen"* (p. 16 [22]).

All this conducts the *Einführung* back to the *Rectorship Address*, and again to the thematics of resolution (*Entschlossenheit*). This last plays a decisive role, in fact the role of decision itself, in *Sein und Zeit*. The paragraph defining questioning as will to know also reminds us that will itself is a being-resolved (*Entschlossensein*).

Although at least in appearance—the appearance of a less emphatic tone—the *Einführung* begins to mark a political retreat in relation to the *Rectorship Address*, in fact it proposes a kind of *geopolitical* diagnosis, of which all the resources and all the references return to spirit, to spiritual historiality, with its already tried and tested concepts: the fall or decadence (*Verfall*) are *spiritual,* so too force is *spiritual.*

Geopolitical, then: Europe, Russia, and America are named here, which still no doubt means just Europe. But the dimension remains properly geopolitical. Thinking the world is determined as thinking the earth or the planet. Heidegger denounces, then, a "spiritual decadence" (*geistigen Verfall*). Peoples are in the process of losing their last "spiritual forces" through this. This last expression returns often. The *Verfall* of spirit cannot allow itself to be thought other than in its relation to the destiny of being. If, in questioning, the experience of spirit appears proportional to "danger," the German people, "our people," this "metaphysical people" (*das metaphysische Volk*) par excellence, is at once the most spiritual (Heidegger specifies this clearly later on in speaking of language), and the most exposed to danger. For it is caught in a vice (p. 29 [36]), in the middle (*in der Mitte*) between its European neighbors, Russia and America.[5] On it devolves the "great decision" (*die grosse Entscheidung*) which will engage the destiny of Europe, the deployment of "new *spiritual* forces from this middle place" (*neuer geschichtlich* geistiger Kräfte aus der Mitte). Emphasis, *emphase:* the word "spiritual" is again italicized both to mark that the fundamental determination of the relation to being occurs there, and to ward off the possibility of a politics other than *of spirit.* A new commencement is called for. It is called for by the question: "*Wie steht es um das Sein?*" What about Being? And this commencement, which is first a recommencement, consists in repeating (*wiederholen*) our historially spiritual existence (*Anfang unseres geschichtlich-geistigen Daseins*). The "we" of this "our" . . . is the German people. I referred too hastily to a geopolitical *diagnosis,* at the point where the discourse is neither that of knowledge nor clinical or therapeutic. But geopolitics conducts us back again from the earth and the planet to the world and to the world as a world *of spirit.* Geopolitics is none other than a *Weltpolitik* of spirit. The world is not the earth. On the earth arrives an obscuring of the world (*Weltverdüsterung*) (p. 34 [45]): the flight of the gods, the destruction of the earth, the massification of man, the preeminence of the mediocre.

VI

What do we call the world? What is the world if it grows obscure in this manner? Reply: "The world is always a *spiritual* world" (p. 34 [45]).

The word *geistig* is once more italicized. Just recently excluded, "avoided," a little later under tight surveillance, hemmed in, compressed, constrained to use quotation marks, here it is now swelling, exclaimed, acclaimed, magnified, at the head, no doubt, of all the emphasized words.

Then Heidegger immediately adds (it's the very next sentence): "*Das Tier hat keine Welt, auch keine Umwelt,*" the animal has no world, nor any environment. Inevitable consequence: the animal has no spirit since, as we have just read, every world is spiritual. Animality is not *of spirit*. And one ought to draw from this proposition all the consequences which would impose themslves with regard to the determination of man as *animal rationale*. We will not be able to do so here, any more than we shall have time to deploy the analysis which this interpretation of animality would demand. I limit myself to the most indispensable schema. Without rushing towards what might be dogmatic in the form of this proposition, and traditional (one would be almost tempted—wrongly—to say Cartesian) about its content, one can note first the following paradox: at first sight the sentence appears expressly to contradict the three theses lengthily elaborated or problematized, but not refuted (to the contrary) in the lectures from the winter semester of

47

1929–30 in Freiburg, in answer to the question, "What is the world?"

I recall these three theses. 1. The stone is without world (*weltlos*). 2. The animal is poor in world (*weltarm*). 3. Man is world-forming, if one can thus translate *weltbildend*. These theses not only prepare for the question, "What is the world?" They must also reply to a certain question of life: how can the essence of life be accessible and determinable? Biological and zoological sciences presuppose access to the essence of the animal creature, they do not open up that access. This at least is what Heidegger affirms in a classical gesture, subjecting regional knowledge to regional ontologies and the latter to a fundamental ontology, and then disqualifying, on this matter, any logic of the vicious circle or of the dialectic.[1] These theses, then, are presented as "metaphysical" and not scientific (p. 277). Access to this *metaphysical* dimension, in the positive sense in which Heidegger then used the term, is closed just as much for the sciences as for philosophical anthropologies, such as that of Scheler, for example. Sciences and anthropologies must, as such, presuppose, without being able to exhibit it, the animal or human world they make their object.

What does *weltarm* mean? What does this poverty of world mean? We cannot here do justice to Heidegger's patient, laborious, awkward, sometimes aporetical analysis. The word "poverty" (*Armut*) could, but this is only a first appearance, enclose two presuppositions or two hypotheses. On the one hand, that of a *difference of degree* separating indigence from wealth (*Reichtum*). The animal would be poor, man rich in world, and therefore in spirit, since the world is spiritual: less spirit for the animal, more spirit for man. On the other hand, if it is poor in world, the animal must certainly have some world, and thus some spirit, unlike the stone which is without world: *weltlos*. Heidegger rejects purely and simply the first hypothesis, whatever difficulty this implies for the maintenance of this word, strange here, "poverty." The difference he is talking about between poverty and wealth is not one of degree. For precisely because of a difference in essence, the world of the animal—and if the animal is poor in world, and therefore in spirit, one *must* be able to talk about a world of the animal, and therefore of a spiritual world—is not a species or a degree of the human world (p. 294). This poverty is not an indigence, a meagreness of world. It has, without doubt, the sense of a privation (*Entbehrung*), of a lack: the animal does not have enough world, to be sure. But this lack is not to be evaluated as a quantitative relation to the entities of the world. It is not that the animal has a lesser relationship, a more limited access to entities, it has an *other* relationship. We will specify it in a moment. But the difficulties are already piling up between two values incompatible in their "logic": that of lack and that of alterity. The lack of world for the animal is not a pure nothingness, but it must not be referred, on a scale of homogeneous degrees, to a plenitude, or to a non-lack in a heterogeneous order, for example that of man. So what justifies this concept of lack or privation once the animal world is no longer a species of the human world? For though the animal is deprived of world, if then it "has no world," according to the brutal formula of the *Introduction to Metaphysics*, it must be the case that its being-deprived, its not-having of world is absolutely different on the one hand from that of the stone—which has no world but is not deprived of it—and on the other hand from the having-a-world of man.

This analysis, certainly, has the interest of breaking with difference of degree. It respects a difference of structure while avoiding anthropocentrism. But it remains bound to reintroduce the measure of man by the very route it claimed to be withdrawing from that measure—this meaning of lack or privation. This latter is anthropocentric or at least referred to the questioning *we* of *Dasein*. It can appear as such and gain meaning only from a non-animal world, and from *our* point of view. What is more, can one not say just as legitimately that the having-a-world also has for man the signification of some *unheimliche* privation of world, and that these two values are not opposed?

Let's start again. If the animal has no world, and therefore no spiritual world, if it is not of spirit, this not-having-a-world (*Nichthaben von Welt*) has a sense radically different from that of the stone which for its part is without world (*weltlos*) but could not, precisely, be deprived of one. The animal has no world either, because it is deprived of it, but its privation means that its not-having is a mode of having and even a certain relation to having-a-world. The *without* of the *without-world* does not have the same sense and does not bespeak the same negativity, for animal and for stone: privation in one case, pure and simple absence in the other. The animal has a world in the mode of not-having, or, conversely, it is deprived of world because it *can* have a world. Heidegger talks of a "poverty" (or privation) as a form of *not-having* in the *being-able-to-have* (*Armut—Entbehren—als Nichthaben im Habenkönnen*) (§50, p.307). No doubt this being-able, this power or potentiality, does not have the sense of an Aristotelian *dynamis.* It is not a virtuality oriented by a *telos.* But how can one avoid the return of this schema?

The animal *has* and *does not have* a world. The proposition seems contradictory and logically impossible, as Heidegger recognizes (p.293). But he adds that "metaphysics and essentiality have a logic different from that of the sound understanding of man." For reasons we have recognized, and in truth out of wariness of Hegelian Reason, Heidegger is not in a hurry to resolve these contradictions of the understanding on the basis of a speculative and dialectical power of absolute reason. (It would here be necessary, precisely around the problem of animality, to reelaborate the question of Heidegger's relationship to Hegel. Once the differences had been recognized and pointed up, troubling affinities might again show through.) The logical contradiction between the two propositions (the animal does and does not have a world) would mean simply that we have not yet sufficiently elucidated the concept of world—the guiding thread of which we are following here since it is none other than that *of spirit*. Spirituality, Heidegger insists on this, is the name of that without which there is no world. It is therefore necessary to manage to think this knot which laces together the two propositions: the animal has no world, the animal has a world. And therefore the animal has and does not have spirit.

We were just saying that poverty must mark a difference that was qualitative, structural and not quantitative. With the stone, the difference is clear. The stone has no access to entities, it has no experience. As for the animal, it has access to entities but, and this is what distinguishes it from man, it has no access to entities *as such*. This privation (*Entbehrung*) is not that (*Privation*) which Heidegger situates in *Sein und Zeit* (§32, p. 149) within the structure of the "as . . . ," of "something as something" (*die Struktur des Etwas als Etwas*). This structure of the "understanding of the world" (*Weltverstehen*) can or must give rise to an antipredicative and preverbal clarification (*Auslegung*). It is not to be confused with the "as" of the statement. The experience of "privation" which Heidegger describes in this context is not more original than that of "seeing with understanding." Rather, it presupposes it and derives from it. What can be said of *Dasein* in this regard cannot be said of the animal, but the discrepant analogy between these two "privations" remains troubling. The animal can have a world because it has access to entities, but it is deprived of a world because it does not have access to entities *as such* and in their Being. The worker bee, says Heidegger, knows the flower, its color and its scent, but it does not know the flower's stamen *as* a stamen, it does not know the roots, the number of stamens, etc. The lizard, whose time on the rock, in the sun, Heidegger describes laboriously and at length (and it makes one long for Ponge), does not relate to the rock and the sun *as such*, as that with regard to which, precisely, one can put questions and give replies. And yet, however little we can identify with the lizard, we know that it has a relationship with the sun—and with the stone, which itself has none, neither with the sun nor with the lizard.

Let us pick up here on a feature which is more than merely amusing. It seems to me significant and we should dwell more on it if there was time. In *Zur Seinsfrage*, some twenty-five years later, as we know, Heidegger proposes to write the word Being under a line of erasure in the form of a cross (*Kreuzweise Durchstreichung*). This cross did not represent either a negative sign or even a sign at all, but it was supposed to recall the *Geviert*, the fourfold, precisely, as "the play of the world," brought together in its place (*Ort*), at the crossing of the cross. The place, for Heidegger, is always a place of collecting together (*Versammlung*). The lecture on "The Thing" (1950) deciphers in this play of the world—recalled in this way by an erasing of "Being"— the becoming-world of the world, *das Welten von Welt*, the world which is in that it worlds (itself) or makes itself worldly (*Die Welt ist, indem sie weltet*). We know the type and the necessity of this formulation. It means in this case that one cannot derive or think the world starting from anything else but it. But look at this other proposition of crossing-through (*Durchstreichung*) from twenty-five years earlier, and already concerning a certain relation to the Being of the entity. Heidegger writes:

> When we say that the lizard is stretched out on the rock, we should cross through (*durchstreichen*) the word "rock," to indicate that while what the lizard is stretched out on is doubtless given him in *some way* (*irgendwie*, italicized), but is not known [or recognized] *as* (*als*, italicized) rock. The crossing-through does not

only mean: something else is apprehended, as something else, but: it is above all not accessible *as entity* (*überhaupt nicht als Seiendes zugänglich*). (pp. 291–92)

Erasure of the name, then, here of the name of the rock which would designate the possibility of naming the rock itself, *as such* and accessible in its being-rock. The erasing would mark in *our* language, by avoiding a word, this inability of the animal to name. But this is first of all the inability to open itself to the *as such* of the thing. It is not of the rock *as such* that the lizard has experience. That is why the name of the rock must be erased when we want to designate what the lizard is stretched out upon. Elsewhere, later, in a text cited by Michel Haar:[2] "The leap from the animal that lives to man that speaks is as great, if not greater, than that from the lifeless stone to the living being." This inability to name is not primarily or simply linguistic; it derives from the properly *phenomenological* impossibility of speaking the phenomenon whose phenomenality as such, or whose very *as such*, does not appear to the animal and does not unveil the Being of the entity. In the language of *Sein und Zeit* (§ 31), one would say that it is a matter of a privation *of* Weltverstehen, not *in* Weltverstehen. Here the erasure of the name would signify the non-access to the entity as such. In being written or not at all being written (for in crossing-through, Heidegger lets what he crosses through be read and he says in this very place that one "ought" to cross through, but he doesn't, as if he were crossing-through the crossing-through, avoiding avoidance, avoiding without avoiding), it is as if, for the animal lacking access to the entity as such, the latter, i.e. the Being of the entity, were crossed out in advance, but with an absolute crossing-out, that of privation. And one can indeed talk of crossing-through, for there is privation of what, thus, should or could be accessible. One does not speak of privation or crossing-through for the stone. But—I repeat, to emphasize both the subtlety of the analysis and the difficulty signaled by this equivocation of terminology—we must distinguish the animal's privation (*Entbehrung*) from Dasein's privation (*Privation*) in comprehension of the world. On the other hand, because of an enigmatic chiasmus which crosses out the crossing-through, the *Durchstreichung* in question here has a sense radically different from that which obliterates the word "Being" in *Zur Seinsfrage*. What is signaled by this animal crossing-through, if we can call it that? Or rather, what is signaled by the word "crossing-through" which we write a propos of the animal "world" and which ought, in its logic, to overtake all words from the moment they say something about the world? The crossing-through recalls a benumbedness (*Benommenheit*) of the animal. Heidegger proposes a description of this which is patient but, it seems to me, awkward. Benumbedness seems to close off access to the entity as such. In truth it does not even close it off, since closure implies opening or aperity, an *Offenbarkeit* to which the animal does not even have access. It would be necessary to cross through the word "closure" too. One cannot say that the animal is closed to the entity. It is closed to the very opening of the entity (p. 361, for example). It does not have access to the difference between the open and the closed.

However problematic, however aporetical even, these theses remain, for us but also for Heidegger who seems to recognize the fact, for example at the end of §63, their strategy and axiomatics will remain remarkably constant. It is always a matter of marking an absolute limit between the living creature and the human *Dasein*, of taking a distance not only from all biologism and even all philosophy of life (and thus from all political ideology which might draw its inspiration more or less directly from them) but also, as Michel Haar rightly recalls, from a Rilkean thematics which links openness and animality. Not to mention Nietzsche, but we'll come back to that in a moment.

We must no doubt recognize, right down to details, the force and necessity of principle in these analyses which break with anthropomorphism, biologism and its political effects, while allowing for the subtle but decisive phenomenal structure of the "as such." It seems to me, however, that they founder on essential difficulties. It could be shown that everything in them still comes down to what the word "spirit" means, to the semantics which regulates the use of this term. If the world is always a spiritual world, as Heidegger never stops repeating in the *Introduction to Metaphysics*; if, as Heidegger also recognizes at the end of these analyses, the three theses, but especially the middle one, remain problematical so long as the concept of world has not been clarified, this is indeed because the spiritual character of the world itself remains obscure. Now let us not forget that it is in connection with the analysis of the world, and as an essential predicate of the world, that the word "spirit" breaks free, if I can put it like that, of its quotation marks, and ought to carry beyond the epoch of Cartesian-Hegelian subjectity. So much so that we should now have to say of spirit what one says of the world for the animal: the animal is poor in spirit, it has spirit but does not have spirit and this not-having is a mode of its being-able-to-have spirit. On the other hand, if privative poverty indeed marks the caesura or the heterogeneity between non-living and living on the one hand, between the animal and human *Dasein* on the other, the fact remains that the very negativity, the residue of which can be read in this discourse on privation, cannot avoid a certain anthropocentric or even humanist teleology. This is a schema which the determination of the humanity of man on the basis of *Dasein* can no doubt modify, displace, shift—but not destroy.

In speaking of teleology, I am not imputing to Heidegger the concept of a progress conceived in evolutionist fashion, of a long march orienting the animal world towards the human world along a scale of beings. But, whether one wishes to avoid this or not, the words "poverty" and "privation" imply hierarchization and evaluation. The expression "poor in world" or "without world," just like the phenomenology supporting it, encloses an axiology regulated not only upon an ontology but upon the possibility of the *onto-logical* as such, upon the ontological difference, the access to the Being of the entity, then the crossing-through of the crossing-through, i.e. opening to the play of the world and first of all to the world of man as *weltbildend*. I do not mean to criticize this humanist teleology. It is no doubt more urgent to recall that, in spite of all the denegations or all the avoidances one could wish, it has remained *up till now* (in Heidegger's time and situation, but this has not radically changed today) the price to be paid in the ethico-political denunciation of biologism, racism, naturalism, etc. If I analyze this "logic," and the aporias or limits, the presuppositions or the axiomatic decisions, above all the inversions and contaminations, in which we see it becoming entangled, this is rather in order to exhibit and then formalize the terrifying mechanisms of this program, all the double constraints which structure it. Is this unavoidable? Can one escape this program? No sign would suggest it, at least neither in "Heideggerian" discourses nor in "anti-Heideggerian" discourses. Can one transform this program? I do not know. In any case, it will not be avoided all at once and without reconnoitering it right down to its most tortuous ruses and most subtle resources.

What are the symptoms that this situation now lets us read in Heidegger's text? If the analysis put forward indeed brings out that the animal is not in the human world in the mode of *Vorhandenheit* (p. 402), any more than the entity is in general for the animal in the mode of *Vorhandenheit*, then one no longer knows what modality of Being to reserve for the animal—for itself and for us, for the human *Dasein*. There is no animal *Dasein*, since *Dasein* is characterized by access to the "as such" of the entity and to the correlative possibility of questioning. It is clear that the animal can be after a prey, it can calculate, hesitate, follow or try out a track, but it cannot properly question. In the same way, it can use things, even instrumentalize them, but it cannot gain access to a *tekhnè*. Allow me to note in passing that three of my guiding threads lace together in this knot: the *question*, the *animal*, *technology*.[3]

But as, on the other hand, the animal is not a *Dasein*, nor is it *Vorhandensein* or *Zuhandensein* for us, as the original possibility of a *Mitsein* with it is not seriously envisaged, one cannot think it or talk of it in terms of *existential* or of *categorical*, to go back to the pair of concepts which structure the existential analytic of *Sein und Zeit*. Can one not say, then, that the whole deconstruction of ontology, as it is begun in *Sein und Zeit* and insofar as it unseats, as it were, the Cartesian-Hegelian *spiritus* in the existential analytic, is here threatened in its order, its implementation, its conceptual apparatus, by what is called, so obscurely still, the animal? Compromised, rather, by a *thesis* on animality which presupposes—this is the irreducible and I believe dogmatic hypothesis of the thesis—that there is one thing, one domain, one homogeneous type of entity, which is called animality *in general*, for which any example would do the job. This is a thesis which, in its *median* character, as clearly emphasized by Heidegger (the animal *between* the stone and man), remains fundamentally teleological and traditional, not to say dialectical.

These difficulties—such at least is the proposition I submit for discussion—never disappear from Heidegger's discourse. They bring the consequences of a serious mortgaging to weigh upon the whole of his thought. And this mortgage indeed finds its greatest concentration in the obscurity of what Heidegger calls spirit.

VII

But as to what is guiding or inspiring Heidegger here, is it possible to distinguish between the obscurity of the concept or the word *Geist* and the obscurity of spirit itself? Correlatively, is it possible to distinguish between the obscurity of the concept or the word *Geist* and the obscurity of spirit itself? Correlatively, is it possible to distinguish between the obscurity of the concept of world and the obscurity, even the darkening, of the world itself (*Weltverdüsterung*), if the world is always "world of spirit"? Perhaps it is preferable to speak here of *darkening* rather than of *obscuring*. This last word [*obscurcissement*], chosen by Gilbert Kahn for the French translation, risks remaining too intellectual and pointing, in the style of Descartes or Valéry, towards what can affect the clarity of the idea. Precisely because it has to do with the world (*Weltverdüsterung*) and not with the idea or even with reason; because, in the *profundity* of a more romantic pathos, by its appeal to the foundations (*Gründen*) and the "profundities" (*Tiefe*), this essay on spiritual *Führung* does not however give "rules for the direction of spirit" (*ad directionem ingenii*), perhaps the word "darkening" is more suitable for it.

The question seems unavoidable, and precisely in this form. For in the passage from the *Einführung* which we took as our starting point just now, Heidegger was meditating first of all on the darkening of the world itself, and thus of spirit. If the concept of world and that of spirit, which is inseparable from it, remain obscure, is this not because the world and spirit are themselves—historically—darkened? Darkened for man and not for animals? There is an *Entmachtung* of spirit. It corresponds to this darkening of the world. It renders spirit destitute by depriving it of its power or its force (*Macht*), of its dynasty. I shall translate *Entmachtung* by "destitution" from now on, because spirit thereby loses a *power* which is not "natural." Such a loss has nothing to do with animal benumbedness. It is exactly at the moment when he is beginning to elucidate this destitution of spirit that Heidegger declares, in the passage cited just now, that "animals have no world":

> What does "world" mean when we are speaking of the darkening of the world? The world is always world *of spirit* (geistige *Welt*). Animals have no world, nor do they have a world-environment. The darkening of the world implies this *destitution* (*Entmachtung*) of spirit, its dissolution, consuming, its repression, and its misinterpretation (*Auflösung, Auszehrung, Verdrängung und Missdeutung*). We are attempting at present to elucidate (*verdeutlichen*) this destitution of spirit from *just one* perspective, and precisely *that* of the misinterpretation of spirit. We have said: Europe is caught in a vice between Russia and America, which metaphysically come down to the same thing in regard to their belonging to the world [to the character of their world, or rather to their character-of-world, *Weltcharakter*] and their relation to spirit (*Verhältnis zum Geist*). The situation of Europe is all the more fatal in that the destitution of spirit derives from Europe itself, and—even if it has been prepared for by something before—was definitively determined, on the basis of Europe's own spiritual situation (*aus seiner eigenem geistigen Lage*), in the first half of the nineteenth century. In our country in this period there occurred what we like to designate in the summary phrase "the collapse (*Zusammenbruch*) of German idealism." This formula is, so to speak, the shield behind which take refuge the already

commenced vacancy of spirit (*die schon anbrechende Geistlosigkeit*), the dissolution of spiritual forces (*die Auflösung der geistigen Mächte*), the refusal of any originary questioning (*alles ursprünglichen Fragens*) of the foundations (*Gründen*), and, finally, our attachment to all those things. For it is not German Idealism which has collapsed, it was the age (*Zeitalter*) which was not strong (*stark*) enough to remain equal to the grandeur, the breadth, and the original authenticity (*Ursprünglichkeit*) of this spiritual world, that is, to realize it (*verwirklichen*) truly, which means something quite different from simply applying maxims and ideas ("points of view": *Einsichten*). *Dasein* has begun to slide in a world without the depth (*Tiefe*) from which, each time in a new way, the essential comes to man and comes back towards him, and thus forces him into a superiority that allows him to act in distinguished fashion. All things are fallen to the same level [. . .] The predominant dimension has become that of extension and number. (pp. 34–35 [45–6])

This discourse on the destitution of spirit calls for some remarks of principle.

1. It is not a discourse on *crisis*. No doubt Heidegger appeals to a historial *decision* supposing the experience of a *krinein*. No doubt he also wants to awaken Europe and philosophy to their responsibility before the task of the question and the originary question of grounds. No doubt he is suspicious, in the first instance, that a certain techno-scientific objectivity represses and forgets the question. No doubt Husserl too asks himself, "How is the spiritual configuration of Europe (*die geistige Gestalt Europas*) characterised?"[1] And yet Heidegger's discourse on the destitution of spirit and on the responsibility of Europe remains, despite many non-fortuitous analogies, in spite of the temporal coincidence (1935), radically heterogeneous with respect to the *Crisis of European Sciences and Transcendental Phe-*

nomenology or the *Crisis of European Humanity and Philosophy.* One could even go further: through the appeal Husserl makes to a transcendental subjectivity which remains in the Cartesian tradition—even if sometimes to awaken it against Descartes—this discourse on the crisis might constitute one of the symptoms of the destitution. And if there is a "weakness" of the age to explain the posited "collapse of German Idealism" we were just speaking of, it would, in part, be linked with the Cartesian heritage as interpreted in *Sein und Zeit*, with this non-questioning of Being presupposed by the metaphysics of subjectivity, in particular in Hegel but also in Husserl.

Heidegger would no doubt have denounced the same Cartesian heritage in *The Crisis of Spirit* (1919), that other discourse from the interwar period in which Valéry, in such a different style, wonders whether one can speak of a "degradation" in the history of the European "genius" or "Psyche." Here, too, one cannot overlook the common focus towards which, between 1919 and 1939, the discourses of worry gather or rush headlong: around the same words (Europe, Spirit), if not in the same language. But the perspective would be falsified and the most acute difference missed if certain analogies between all these discourses—troubling and significant, although local—were selected, on the pretext, for example, that Heidegger might have subscribed to such and such a formulation. Thus Valéry asks himself: "Must the phenomenon of exploitation of the globe, the phenomenon of equalization of techniques and the phenomenon of democracy, which allow one to foresee a *diminutio capitis* of Europe, be taken as absolute decisions of destiny? Or have we some freedom *against* this menacing conjuration of things?"[2]

2. If *Entmachtung* dooms spirit to impotence or powerlessness, if it deprives it of its strength and the nerve of its authority (the French translation by Gilbert Kahn has "en-

ervation" of spirit) what does this mean as far as force is concerned? That spirit *is* a force and *is not* a force, that it has and has not power. If it were force in itself, if it were force itself, it would not lose force, there would be no *Entmachtung*. But if it were not this force or power, the *Entmachtung* would not affect it essentially, it would not be *of spirit*. So one can say neither the one nor the other, one must say both, which doubles up each of the concepts: world, force, spirit. The structure of each of these concepts is marked by the relation to its double: a relation of haunting. A haunting which allows neither analysis nor decomposition nor dissolution into the simplicity of a perception. And it is because there is doubling that *Entmachtung* is possible—only *possible*, since a ghost does not exist and offers itself to no perception. But this possibility is sufficient to make the destitution of spirit a priori inevitable [*fatale*]. When one says of spirit or of the spiritual world that it both has and does not have force—whence the haunting and the double—is it only a matter of contradictory utterances? Of that contradiction of the understanding at which thought should not come to a halt, as Heidegger said of the animal which both has and does not have the world, spirit, the question? Would the ghost vanish before thought like a mirage of the understanding, or even of reason?

3. Heidegger says that destitution is a movement *proper* to spirit, proceeding from within it. But this inside must also enclose the spectral duplicity, an immanent outside or an intestine exteriority, a sort of evil genius which slips into spirit's monologue to haunt it, ventriloquizing it and thus dooming it to a sort of self-persecuting disidentification. Moreover, a little later in the same passage, Heidegger names the demonic. Evidently not the Evil Genius of Descartes (which is, however, in German *böse Geist*). The hyperbolical hypothesis of the Evil Genius, *to the contrary*, gives way precisely before that which constitutes evil for

Heidegger, the one who haunts spirit in all the forms of its destitution: the certainty of the *cogito* in the position of the *subjectum* and therefore absence of originary questioning, scientific methodologism, leveling, predominance of the quantitative, of extension and of number—so many motifs which are "Cartesian" in type. All of that, which accepts lie and destruction, is evil, the foreigner: foreign to spirit *in* spirit. When Heidegger names the demonic (*Einführung*, p. 35 [46]), he specifies, in a brief parenthesis: in the sense of destructive malignity (*im Sinne des zerstörerisch Bösartigen*). Spiritual essence of evil. Some of Heidegger's formulations here are literally Schellingian. We shall meet them again in the text on Trakl which includes at its center a thinking of evil as torment *of* spirit. The "spiritual night," or the "spiritual (*geistliche*) twilight" (expressions of Trakl's that Heidegger will want to remove from the metaphysics of *Geistigkeit* as well as from the Christian value of *Geistlichkeit*—a word which will itself thus find itself doubled) are not without their profound relationship with what is said twenty years earlier of the darkening of world and spirit. Just as the *Entmachtung* of spirit is not without relationship, in the *Introduction to Metaphysics*, with the decomposition of man, or rather—we shall come to this—with the "*verwesende Geslecht*," the *O des Menschen verweste Gestalt* of Trakl as Heidegger will interpret it in *Unterwegs zur Sprache.*

The destitution of spirit is thus a *self*-destitution, a resignation. But it must be that an other than spirit, still itself however, affects and divides it. This Heidegger does not say, at least in this form, even though, it seems to me, it must imply the return of this double when he speaks of the demonic.

4. The resignation of spirit produces, and produces itself as, *Umdeutung* and *Missdeutung:* as difference or interpretative mutation,and also as misinterpretation of the mean-

ing of spirit, of spirit itself. We cannot here go through the several pages analyzing the four great types of *Um-* and *Missdeutungen*. But each word would be worth it.

a) There is first the resignation of spirit into intelligence (*Intelligenz*), understanding (*Verständigkeit*), calculation (*Berechnung*), mass distribution (*massenhafte Verteilung*), the reign of the literati and the aesthetes, of what is "merely spiritual" (*das* Nur-*Geistreiche:* in the sense of wit, of being clever). What has pretensions to be an intellectual culture of spirit thus manifests only a simulacrum and lack of spirit. Needless to say, the form of the propositions I was advancing just now (paradoxes, discursive contradictions—and thus a structure of haunting) would in Heidegger's eyes betray the same resignation of spirit before the calculating authority of the understanding. Must I specify that I would not subscribe to this diagnosis? Without suggesting a different one, all I am doing or trying to do here is to begin to think through— I will not even say to question—the axiomatics of this diagnosis, the status it assigns to the understanding in what is still an extremely Hegelian way, and that includes the imperative, or even the "piety," of questioning. We will return to this later on.

b) Secondly, there is the instrumentalization of spirit. Like Bergson, and at least on this point (and we know now that Heidegger read him more than his texts would lead one to think), Heidegger here associates intelligence (*Intelligenz*), that falsification of spirit, with the instrument (*Werkzeug* and instrumentalization. Marxism is named twice in this paragraph: the transformation of spirit into superstructural or powerless intellect or, symmetrically, if that is the word, the organization of the people as a living mass or a race. Here are a few lines at least to let the tone of this teaching be heard. His target is the cult of the body, in Russia as much as in Germany. I think it was one year before the memorable Berlin Olympic Games in 1936 (again the Greek-German axis and the elevation towards the "gods of the stadium"), during which a *Führer* refused to shake hands with Jesse Owens, the black sprinter:

> Every true force and true beauty of the body, every sure aim and boldness of the sword (*Kühnheit des Schwertes*), but also every authenticity (*Echtheit*) and every ingeniousness of understanding—all are founded in spirit, and find their elevation (*Erhöhung*) and their fall (*Verfall*) only in the power or the powerlessness of spirit (*Macht und Ohnmacht des Geistes*). (p. 36 [47])

c) When the spiritual world resigns before the instrument, it becomes culture or civilization (*Kultur*). To explain this, Heidegger cites his inaugural lecture of 1929 ("What is Metaphysics?"). He takes from it this passage distinguishing between the bad unity of the university, technical and administrative unity, whose unity is only nominal, and *truly* spiritual unity. Only this last is a true *unity*, for what is *proper* to spirit is, precisely, to unify. In outlining what the university lacks, Heidegger gives a definition of spirit which will not, I think, shift throughout the rest of his work: "*eine ursprünglich einigende, verpflichtende geistige Macht*," a spiritual power which originally unites and engages, assigns, obliges.

d) Fourth form of resignation: the reference to spirit can become a theme of cultural propaganda or political maneuver, especially when Russian communism changes tactics and invokes spirit in its support after having campaigned against it. Heidegger's argument appears terribly equivocal at this point: *mutatis mutandis*, what about his own tactics—and these tactics are also political—when they change, moving from a deconstruction to a celebration of spirit?

After denouncing this fourth misinterpretation, Heidegger again defines spirit, this time citing the *Rectorship Address*. But what is it that now becomes spectacular in this quotation? Discreetly spectacular enough, however, for no attention ever to have been paid it?[3] The silent play of the quotation marks. For we are taking seriously what is being played for in this play. We are still interested in this dramaturgy—which is also a pragmatics—of signals for reading, and in what is at stake in these typographical marionettes, in this sleight of hand, this handwriting that is artisanal and so agile. The hand calculates very fast. Silently it contrives, apparently without contrivance, the instantaneous alternation of a *fort/da*, the sudden appearance, then disappearance of these little aphonic forms which say and change everything according as one shows or hides them. And when one puts them away after exhibiting them, one can speak of a repression, a suppression, others would say a denegation, let us say a *bringing to heel* [*mise au pas*]. The operation is properly *conducted*, conducted by a master's hand. I recall that in German "quotation mark" is *Anführungsstriche* or *Anführungszeichen. Anführen*, to conduct, to take the head, but also to dupe, to make fun of [*se payer la tête*] or brainwash somebody.

What is spectacular here? No doubt this: on this one occasion, the suppression—one dare not say the censorship—of the quotation marks operates within the quotation of an *already* published text—a text by the same author, the only published version of which includes quotation marks, the very ones which the quotation, of the same author by the same author, suddenly removes. In the definition of spirit put forward in the *Rectorship Address*, the quotation marks still remained, an already quite exceptional residue. They disappear in the quotation given in the *Introduction to Metaphysics* two years later.

This is the only modification, and Heidegger does not point it out. And yet he goes so far as to indicate the number of the page he has just quoted from the *Rectorship Address*. One must therefore be extremely curious to notice a revision thus passed over in silence. It operates, perhaps with the lucidity of inadvertence, like the erasure of one remorse by another: invisible crossing-out, scarcely perceptible crossing-out of what already—as quotation marks always do—sketches the polite movement of a crossing-out. Here then is the definition of spirit (open the quotation marks for the quotation, lift the quotation marks around *Geist* in the quotation thus "actualized"):

> Spirit [in quotation marks in the *Address*] is neither empty sagacity, nor the gratuitous game of joking, nor the unlimited work of analysis of the understanding, nor even the reason of the world, but spirit [here the quotation marks had already been removed in the *Address*] is the being-resolved [or the determined opening: *Entschlossenheit*] to the essence of Being, of a resolution which accords with the tone of the origin and which is knowledge.[4]

How to awaken spirit? How to lead it out of *resignation* [*démission*] to responsibility? By calling it back to the care of the question of Being and in the same movement, in it, to the taking charge of the sending (*Sendung*), of a *mission*, the historial mission of *our people*, as the middle of the West:

> Spirit is the full power given to the potencies of entities as such and in totality (*die Ermächtigung der Mächte des Seienden als solchen im Ganzen*). Where spirit reigns (*herrscht*), the entity as such becomes always and on every occasion more entity (*seiender*). This is why the questioning toward entities as such in totality, the questioning of the question of Being, is one of the fundamental questions for a reawakening of spirit (*Erweckung des Geistes*), and thereby for the originary world of a historial *Dasein*, and thereby to master the danger of a darkening of the world, and thereby for a taking up of the historial mission (*geschichtliche Sendung*) of our people, inasmuch as it is the middle of the West. (p. 38 [48])

The awakening of spirit, the reappropriation of its potency, thus passes, once more, through the responsibility of questioning, as it is entrusted, assigned, destined to "our people." The fact that the same chapter should, in its conclusion, open onto the destiny of language (*Schicksal der Sprache*) in which is grounded the relation (*Bezug*) of a people to Being, shows clearly enough that all these responsibilities are interwoven: that of our people, that of the question of Being, and that of our language. Now at the beginning of the chapter on the grammar of the word "be," it is again the *spiritual* quality which defines the absolute privilege of the German language.

Why this incommensurable privilege of one language? And why is this privilege determined with regard to spirit? What would the "logic" of this be, if one can still speak of logic in a region wherein is decided the originarity of language in general [*le langage*] and a given language [*langue*]?

The "logic" justifying such a privilege is strange, naturally unique, but also irrefutable and entrusted to a sort of paradoxy, the formality of which would be worth long developments. According to one's mood, it calls forth either the most serious or the most amused reflections. (That's what I like about Heidegger. When I think about him, when I read him, I'm aware of both these vibrations at the same time. It's always horribly dangerous and wildly funny, certainly grave and a bit comical.) In the well-known passage I am going to quote, I shall emphasize two features which have perhaps not been given all the necessary attention:

> The fact that the formation (*Ausbildung*) of western grammar should be due to Greek reflection (*Besinnung*) on the *Greek* language gives this process all its significance. For this language is, along with German (*neben der deutschen*) (from the point of view of the possibilities of thinking), both the most powerful of all, and the most spiritual (*geistigste*). (p. 43 [57]).

Two features to emphasize, then, and two very odd *dissymmetries*.

1. The first dissymmetry unbalances the relationship between Greek and German on the one hand, all the languages of the world on the other. Heidegger does not just mean to recall that one always thinks in a language and that whoever affirms this must still do so in his or her language without the ability or the duty to place himself or herself in some metalinguistic neutrality. For one must indeed sign this theorem in one's own language. Such a signature is never individual. It commits, via the language, a people or a community. No, such a proposition, which could correspond to a sort of linguistico-cultural, anthropological relativism—all communities think and think equally in their language—does not correspond to Heidegger's thinking. It does not correspond, he would say, with *thought*, insofar as thought *corresponds* uniquely with Being and can correspond with Being only according to the singular event of a language capable of naming, of calling up Being—or, rather, of hearing itself called by Being.

That the joint privilege of German and Greek is absolute here with regard to thought, to the question of Being, and thus to spirit, is implied by Heidegger everywhere. But in the interview with *Der Spiegel*, he says it in a calmly arrogant way, perhaps a bit naively, at once on his guard and defenseless and, I would say, in "our" language, *sans beaucoup d'esprit*. Faced with such opinionating, it is tempting to add a very Latin exclamation mark to my title: *de l'esprit*, what the devil! (return of the devil in a moment, and of the double at the heart of *Geist*).

This then is a certain Heidegger, when the mike or *Der Spiegel* is held up to him:

> I am thinking of the special relationship, inside the German language, with the language of the Greeks and their thought. It is something which the French are always confirming for me today. When they begin to think, they speak German: they say definitely that they would not manage it in their language.[5]

One imagines the scene of these confidences, or rather of this "confirmation." Heidegger certainly did not make it up: "they" go to complain about their language to the master and, one supposes, in the master's language. In its abyssal depth, this declaration is not necessarily without truth—it even becomes a truism if one accepts a fundamental axiomatics according to which the meaning of *Geist, Denken, Sein,* and a few other words cannot be translated and so can be thought only in German, even if one is French. What else can one say and think in German? But the dogmatic assurance, aggravated by the discourteous tone of a declaration which is literally invasive, as much in what it says as in what it shows, would in itself be enough to raise certain doubts about it. The insolence is not even provocative; it is half asleep in tautology. Fichte said some analogous things, in the name of the same "logic," in his *Address to the German Nation:* he who thinks and thus wishes for "spirituality" in its "freedom" and in its "eternal progress," is German, he is one of us (*ist unsers Geschlechts*), wherever he was born and whatever language he speaks. Conversely, he who does not think and does not wish for such a "spirituality," even if he was born German and seems to speak German, even if he has so-called linguistic competence in German, "he is non-German and foreign for us" (*undeutsch und fremd für uns*), and it is to be wished that he separate himself from us totally."[6]

2. This break with relativism is not, however, a eurocentrism. There would be several ways of demonstrating this. One of them would consist in recalling that it is not eurocentric in virtue of this first raising of the stakes: it is a central-europo-centrism. For another dissymmetry will come along one day, precisely at the place of *Geist,* and burst open the Graeco-German axis. Twenty years later, Heidegger will have to suggest, in short, that the Greek language has no word to say—nor therefore, to translate—*Geist:* at least a certain *Geistlichkeit,* if not the *Geistigkeit* of *Geist.* The

Greek language: in other words the language of philosophy as well as that of the Gospels. For while Heidegger seems to concede, in a reading of Schelling, and from Schelling's point of view, that *Geist*, which in any case has never been *Spiritus*, at least names the same thing as *pneuma*,[7] in his *Gespräch* with Trakl, he affirms that *Geist* and *geistlich* in Trakl refer *first of all* to flame and not to breath or pneumatic inspiration. The adjective *geistlich* would thus lose even the connotation of Christian spirituality by which it is normally opposed to the secular or to metaphysical *Geistigkeit*. The *Geist* of this *Geistlichkeit* could be thought only in *our language*.

It turns out then that of the two twinned languages, Greek and German, which have in common the greatest spiritual richness, only one of them can name what they have and are in common par excellence: spirit. And to name is to offer for thinking. German is thus the only language, at the end of the day, at the end of the race, to be able to name this maximal or superlative (*geistigste*) excellence which in short it shares, finally, *only up to a certain point* with Greek. In the last instance, it is the only language in which spirit comes to name itself. In the last instance, in the last place: for this separation between *Geist* and *pneuma* will be marked only in 1953, at the moment when the difference between *geistig* and *geistlich* will also be marked and then, within *geistlich*, the difference between the traditional Christian meaning and a more originary meaning. But in 1935, in the *Introduction to Metaphysics*, what Greek and German have in common is still the greatest *geistigkeit*, the one that in 1953 will be defined (in reality denounced) as a Platonic inheritance.

There too, the violence of the dissymmetry should not come as a surprise. It too comes very close to truism or tautology. To say, as Heidegger is still doing in the *Introduction*, that the privilege *shared* by Greek and German is that of *Geist* is *already* to interrupt the sharing and accentuate once more the dissymmetry. One cannot ask for the Greek's approval. If s/he had given it, s/he would at least have done so in his or her language. S/he would have said: yes, *Pneuma*, sure, our two languages, from the point of view of the possibility of thinking (*noein?*), are the most pneumatic or pneumatological. S/he would have perhaps used other words too, but would not have failed to claim the prerogative of Greek, the only one to be able to say and think that. More likely, in the logic of this fabulous truism,[8] one can bet that the Greek would not have dreamed for a moment, and for good reason, of associating German with this claim. Not for an instant, not even provisionally, as Heidegger still does in 1935.

VIII

During the same years, as we know, the strategy of interpretation also concerns Nietzsche. It is supposed to withdraw him from any biologistic, zoologistic, or vitalistic reappropriation. This strategy of interpretation is also a politics.
The extreme ambiguity of the gesture consists in saving a
body of thought by damning it. One unearths in it a metaphysics, the last metaphysics, and orders all the significa-
tions of Nietzsche's text according to it. As in Hegel, we
would still apparently be dealing with a metaphysics of absolute subjectity. But unconditioned subjectity is here no
longer that of the willing which *knows itself*, i.e. that of
spirit, but the absolute subjectity of the body, of impulsions
and affects: the unconditioned subjectity of the will to
power. The history of modern metaphysics, which determines the essence of man as *animal rationale*, divides as
follows. There are two symmetrical sides to unconditioned
subjectity: rationality as spirit on the one hand, animality as
body on the other:

> By virtue of this fact, the unconditioned essence of
> subjectity necessarily unfolds as *brutalitas* of *bestiali-
> tas*. [. . .] *Homo est brutum bestiale.*[1]

But we should think this thing that Nietzsche calls "the
blond beast" metaphysically, without rushing towards a philosophy of life, towards a vitalism or a biologism, without
conferring the meanings "vital" or "biological" on the totality of entities. It would be necessary to do the opposite,

which is also something quite different: to reinterpret the vital on the basis of the will to power. This "has nothing 'vital' or 'spiritual' about it: to the contrary, the 'vital' (the 'living') and the 'spiritual' are, as belonging to entities, determined by Being in the sense of the Will to power" (vol II, p. 300 [III, 224]).

In the same way, the thought of race (*Rassengedanke*) is interpreted in metaphysical and not biological terms (vol. II, p. 309 [III, 231]). By thus inverting the direction of determination, is Heidegger alleviating or aggravating this "thought of race"? Is a metaphysics of race more or less serious than a naturalism or a biologism of race? Let us leave the question of this still equivocal strategy suspended too.

On this view, Nietzsche would not therefore be proposing a philosophy of life or a Darwinian explanation of rationality, and therefore of spirit in the Hegelian sense, that other part of the rational animal. Heidegger nonetheless takes issue with those for whom the spirit, according to Nietzsche, would be " 'the soul's adversary', and therefore the adversary of life" ("*Geist als Widersacher der Seele,*" *d.h. des Lebens*) (vol. I, p. 581 [III, 93]). No, Nietzsche does not disavow or deny spirit, he does not avoid it. Spirit is not the adversary (*Widersacher*) but the scout (*Schrittmacher*)—it draws and, once again, *leads* the soul whose path it breaks. When it opposes soul, i.e. life, when it does this harshly, this is in favor and not to the detriment of life.

Spirit/soul/life, pneuma/psyché/zoè or *bios, spiritus/anima/vita, Geist/Seele/Leben*—these are the triangles and squares in which we imprudently pretend to recognize stable semantic determinations, and then to circumscribe or skirt round the abysses of what we ingenuously call translation. Later we shall wonder what the opening of these angles might mean. And primarily what goes on between spirit and *psyché*.

The relationship of spirit to soul would situate the focal

point, so to speak, of those 1942 lectures collected under the title "The Essence of the Poet as Demigod," and especially in the chapter devoted to "the spirit which grounds historially" (*Der geschichtlich gründende Geist*).[2] The attempt is to elucidate some lines by Hölderlin published by Beissner in 1933:

> nemlich zu Hauss ist der Geist
> nicht im Anfang, nicht an der Quell. Ihn zehret die Heimath.
> Kolonie liebt, und tapfer Vergessen der Geist.
> Unsere Blumen erfreun und die Schatten unserer Wälder
> den Verschmachteten. Fast wäre der Beseeler verbrandt.

I shall not venture to translate these few lines, especially not the first two whose syntax, the place and intonation of the "nicht," have been for quite a while now the subject of a debate which it is perhaps not indispensable to get involved in here.

"Who is the 'spirit'?" asks Heidegger (p. 157). Who is the spirit who "*zu Hauss ist . . . /nicht im Anfang, nicht an der Quell . . .*"?

At that time, he explains, the word "spirit" has a univocal meaning, even if it is not fully developed. Hölderlin gets this essential meaning from the thought of Hegel and Schelling. But one would go astray if one concluded that Hölderlin *borrowed* the metaphysical concept of spirit to take it on here or there in poetry. First, a poet, and a poet of Hölderlin's rank, does not *borrow*, does not *take on* something like a "concept." Secondly, his poetic *Auseinandersetzung* with metaphysical thought leads him to send it packing, to "overcome" it in this very relationship. Even if his word *Geist* lets itself be determined by German metaphysics, it is not identical with it, it cannot be reduced to what German metaphysics thinks, in systematic mode, in its concepts of subjective or objective spirit.[3] For these metaphysical systems, the *Geist* is the unconditioned absolute which determines and *gathers* every entity. It is thus, as spirit, the "gemeinsame *Geist*," the spirit of gathering (rather than common spirit). In its metaphysical concept, inasmuch as it gathers, spirit is, par excellence, thought, thinking itself (*Denken*). It is properly (*eigentlich*), it is truly spirit inasmuch as, thinking the essential, it gathers—which it does by *thinking itself*, thus finding itself at home, *close up to itself* (*zu Hauss*). Its thoughts do not simply belong to it, they are—and this is Hölderlin's line of verse—thoughts of the spirit which gathers into community:

des gemeinsamen Geistes Gedanken sind.

One should not read in this a metaphysical proposition "astray" in a poem. The hymn poetically meditates spirit as what is; and what is assigns to every entity the sending or the mission of its Being. This assignment or mission is spoken all along the chain of *Geschick, Schickliche, Schicksal, Geschichte,* whose untranslatability is not foreign to the fact that the language in which the chain is deployed is itself the *proper place* or even the irreplaceable idiom of this assigning mission, of this sending of history itself. Given that man has a privileged relationship to the entity as such, his opening to what is sent—dispensed, destined—to him confers on him an essential *Geschichtlichkeit*. This is what allows him to be and to have a history.

Let us suppose that this interpretation of spirit—that which *gathers* or in which what gathers is gathered—is not in fact a metaphysical proposition *astray* in the poem. It will still be necessary to take seriously at least two obvious things. On the one hand, Heidegger's formulation is the same, whether he is dealing, ten years later, with spirit in the work of Trakl which he also wants to withdraw from pneumatology or metaphysical and Christian spirituality, or whether—some years before these lectures on Hölderlin—

with the course on Schelling (*Treatise of 1809 on the Essence of Human Freedom*). This course emphasizes the "unifying" essence of spirit which is "originally unifying unity" (*ursprünglich einigende Einheit*) (p. 154 [p. 128]). With regard to *this* unity, Heidegger writes then: "In that it is a unity, spirit is πνεῦμα" (*Als solche Einheit ist der Geist* πνεῦμα).

What he names then in *das Wehen* (a word which means breath but is never far from suffering or sighing, from the breathless or breathless-making "spiration" of spirit) is only the breath (*Hauch*) or spiration of what properly unites in the most originary fashion: love. But for Schelling, spirit is less high than love, of which it is only the breath. Spirit manifests the breath of love, love in its respiration. It is easier to name (and it also proffers the Verb) than love—love which "was present" (*da war*), if one can say so, before the separation of ground and existent. How is love to be designated? How can we name the Very High of what is above spirit and thus moves spirit, breathes it in or exhales it? How should we designate (*bezeichnen*) it, Schelling asks:

> For even spirit is not yet the Most High; it is only spirit, that is the breath of love. But it is love which is the Most High. It is what was present before ground and existence were (in their separation), all the same it was not yet present as love, but . . . but how can we designate it? (Ibid.)

"Here the 'verb' (*das Wort*) also abandons the thinker," Heidegger then notes. "Here": in this place where it is a question of speaking love, the Most High, the sole and unifying origin of language—in other words, of breathing. "Also" the thinker, because the verb, the word (*das Wort*), is thus the moment of breathing or spirit which at a certain point has no word. For, in that it is language, it cannot go back or raise itself up to name that which set it in motion, before it or higher than it: its origin, love. What Schelling says here (and Heidegger then comments upon), of the infinite desire in God, of separation, of nostalgia (*Sehnsucht*), and of the evil whose possibility is due to the divisibility of *Geist* in man (and not in God) (p. 169)—all this leaves legible traces in the readings of Trakl and, first, of Hölderlin, to whom I return briefly.

That spirit founds history and that the sending remains for man a future, the coming of future [*avenir*] or the to-come [*à-venir*] of a coming: this is what Hölderlin thinks as a poet. And since, in imposing on him this word from the French language, I have spoken a great deal of spirit as a *revenant*, Heidegger would say here, in another language, that it is necessary to think of "returning" [*la revenance*] starting from a thought—always yet to come—of coming. Returning itself remains to come, from the thinking in it of coming, of coming in its very coming. This is what Hölderlin thinks, that of which he has experience and preserves experience as a poet. To be a poet (*dichten*) in this sense is to be dedicated to this experience and this preserving. In that it founds historially, spirit finds its place, it takes place first in the poet, in the soul (*Seele*) of the poet. The soul is here the synonym, an "other word" for "*Mut*" or "*Gemüt.*" *Gemüt* is not spirit, but the poet's *Gemüt* receives, lodges spirit, it gives place in him to the welcoming of spirit, of *Geist*—coming or coming back [*revenant*] in him.

> Das Kommende in seinem Kommen wird erfahren und bewahrt im Dichten. Der geschichtlich gründende Geist muss daher zuerst seine Stätte finden im "Mut" des Dichters. Das andere Wort für das "Gemüt" ist "Seele." (p. 160)

What is missing in the metaphysics of subjectity, we read in *Sein und Zeit*, is a correct interpretation of *Gemüt*. There is no doubt that Heidegger claims to come across it here in listening to Hölderlin.[4] The soul is not the principle of life for animals and plants, but the essence of Gemüt which welcomes to itself the thoughts of spirit:

Des gemeinsamen Geistes Gedanken sind
Still endend in der Seele des Dichters.

The thoughts of spirit inhabit the soul of the poet, they are at home there, native, *heimisch*. The poet gives soul rather than giving life. He is the *Beseeler*, not the animator or the ringleader but the one who insufflates the soul. He gives spirit its space, he makes it reign in what is. By saying what is, he lets it appear in its *Begeisterung*. The *Begeisterung* of the poet, his passion, his enthusiasm—I daren't say his "inspiration" (and like "animator," it is always the Latin word which seems to betray)—opens this saying of spirit: *"Dichten" ist das Sagen der Gedanken des Geistes: Dichten ist dichtender Geist.*

The space of a lecture does not allow an analysis of the reading Heidegger proposes of the lines:

nemlich zu Hauss ist der Geist
nicht im Anfang, nicht an der Quell. Ihn zehret die Heimath.

We should have to listen to Adorno and to Beda Allemann, who have contested this reading. We should also have to take into account the subtle attention Heidegger pays to the *Betonung* (as in *Der Satz vom Grund*), to the different possibilities of marking the tonal accent, for example that of *nicht* in the line I have just quoted (p. 161). I must be content with picking out from this reading the words or the motifs which could guide us in the recognition of a trajectory. This movement follows a sort of limit. Given this, it touches both sides of the limit and makes division almost impossible. It is the limit between a metaphysical thinking of spirit, under which fall the systematic philosophemes of Hegel, of Schelling, but also, for a certain dimension of his saying, of Hölderlin, and, on the other hand, the other handout of this divide, those *Dichter* who are the same Hölderlin, the same but an other, and Trakl.

The words or the motifs which could guide us in this trajectory turn out to be those speaking of the *motif*, the *movement*, the *trajectory*. We are always dealing with a thought not of the circle but of the return, of a turning of the *Rückkehr* towards the home (*Heimat, heimisch, "nemlich zu Hauss"*). It belongs to the essence of spirit that it only *is* properly (*eigentlich*) if it is close to itself [*auprès de soi*]. It is thus that *der gemeinsame Geist* gathers itself. This desire for gathering or re-membering installs in it that nostalgia, that *Sehnsucht*, in which, the course on Schelling reminds us, the term *Sucht* has, etymologically, nothing to do with the *suchen* of research, but with evil, *siech*, illness, epidemic. This evil is inscribed in desire, and, like desire itself, it carries in it a motivity, an "adversed mobility" (gegenwendige *Bewegtheit*): go out of oneself and return into oneself (*Schelling . . . ,* p. 150 [p. 125]). The evil of this *Sehnsucht* which gives the impulsion to go out of oneself in order to return to oneself, or to return to oneself so as to go out of oneself, is the essence of spirit of which Hölderlin speaks as poet. "In spirit," says Heidegger, "there reigns the nostalgia for its own essence." (G, vol. 53, p. 163).

Given this, at the beginning of this expropriation-reappropriation, in this *ex-appropriation*, spirit is never at home. It is on the basis of this sort of originary depropriation that Heidegger interprets

Kolonie liebt, und tapfer Vergessen der Geist.

It loves the colony, and valiant forgetting, Spirit.[5]

We should have to analyze another motif too. All I can do here is to situate it on the same path. The motif of *fire*. It crosses that of return, and Heidegger interprets it through the experience of the Germans between the first line of *Der Ister* which says to the fire "come," "come now!" an apostrophe which, in instituting fire as what comes, as the coming or the future [*avenir*] of what comes, comes itself, the apostrophe, from the fire it calls and which, in a turning, in truth calls for it, will always already have called for it, made the poet speak like the fire:

Jetzt komme, Feuer!

Now come, Oh fire!

—between this and the letter to Böllendorf (4 December 1801) which speaks of a "fire of heaven" originarily as natural to the Greeks as to us the clarity of *Darstellung*.

Hölderlin is he who has been struck by the God of light. "He *is*," says Heidegger, "on the return path (*auf der Rückkehr*) from his walk towards the fire (*von der Wanderung zum "Feuer"*)" (G, vol. 53, p. 170).

And in this sketch of a final stanza for *Bread and Wine*, the last of the five lines which hold Heidegger's attention here names the consumption, the burning, fire, or even the cremation or incineration of the *Beseeler*, of the one who animates, of the one who carries the soul, in other words the gift of the spirit. Hölderlin, the *Beseeler*, is consumed in fire, close to becoming ash:

Unsere Blumen enfreun und die Schatten unserer Wälder den Verschmachten. Fast wäre der Beseeler verbrandt. (Ibid. p. 166)

Our flowers enchant and the shadows of our woods He who consumes himself. He would be almost ash the animator.

Why have I been selective like this in these readings of Schelling and Hölderlin? Why leave the path open to this fire of spirit only? Because one can begin—such at least is my hypothesis—to recognize in it, in its very equivocation[6] or indecision, the edging or dividing path which ought, according to Heidegger, to pass between a Greek or Christian—even onto-theological—determination of *pneuma* or *spiritus*, and a thinking of *Geist* which would be other and more originary. Seized by German idiom, *Geist* would rather, earlier [*plutôt, plus tôt*], give to think flame.

IX

What is spirit?

Everything suggests that, from as early as 1933, the date at which, lifting at last the quotation marks, he begins to talk *of spirit* and in the name *of spirit*, Heidegger never stopped interrogating the Being of *Geist*.

What is spirit? Final reply, in 1953: fire, flame, burning, conflagration.

Twenty years later, then, and what years!

But we are going to speak of the *"year"* (*Jahr*), and precisely in order to approach what "later" sometimes means. What comes very late, the latest, can also lead back closer to an origin, or return [*revenir*], rather, to the origin before the origin, earlier even than the beginning.

The *Gespräch* with Trakl,[1] that collocution of *Denker* and *Dichter*, strikes the reply. Between thinker and poet, *Gespräch* does not signify conversation, as it is sometimes translated, nor dialogue, nor exchange, nor discussion, and still less communication. The speech of the two who speak, the language which speaks *between* them divides and gathers according to a law, a mode, a regime, a genre which can receive their name only from *the very thing* which is said here, by the language or speech of this *Gespräch*. Language speaks *in* speech. It speaks about itself, refers to itself in deferring itself. Here we shall not read a *Gespräch* between Heidegger and Trakl *on the subject of spirit*. The *Gespräch* will be defined as a determinate mode of speech only from what is said of spirit, of the essence of *Geist* as it divides and gathers in conflagration.

What is spirit?

The reply is inscribed in maxims which translate certain poetic statements by Trakl, in a form which one would call ontological if ontology were still the dominant regime of these texts.

"*Doch was ist der Geist?*" Heidegger indeed asks. What is spirit? Reply: "*Der Geist ist das Flammende*" (p. 59 [179]). Further on, "*Der Geist ist Flamme*"(p. 62 [181]).

How to translate? Spirit is what inflames? Rather, what inflames *itself*, setting *itself* on fire, setting fire to *itself?* Spirit is flame. A flame which inflames, or which inflames *itself:* both at once, the one and the other, the one the other. *Con*flagration of the two in the very con*flagration*.

Let us try to bring our language closer to this furnace. A furnace *of* spirit, in that double genitive by which spirit affects, affects *itself* and *gets affected* by fire. Spirit *catches* fire and *gives* fire; let us say that spirit in-flames, in one or two words, both verb and noun. That which both catches (or takes) and gives is fire. The fire of spirit. Let us not forget what was said above and that we are going to re-read once again: spirit gives soul (*psyche*), it does not only give it up in death.

Spirit *in-flames*, how is this to be *heard* or *understood* [*entendre*]? Not: what does it mean? But how does it sound and resound? What about the consonance, the singing, the praise, and the hymn in this *Gespräch* with a poet? And in order to open up this question, perhaps it is necessary to think even that, even those of whom Heidegger said: "Their singing is poetic speech" (*Ihr Singen ist das Dichten*). To which he adds, setting the question going again: how? how much? What does it mean, poetic speech? To what do we give that name? What is so called, so calls? "*Inwiefern? Was heisst Dichten?*"[2]

In this *Gespräch*, there will be no deciding whether the

thinker speaks in his name or in correspondence with Trakl. In the face of such statements, there will be no deciding whether visible or invisible quotation marks, or even some still more subtle marks, must suspend the assigning of a *simple* responsibility. In order to decide, a long meditation would be necessary, before such an assigning, as to what Heidegger says at the beginning about double speech and doubly addressed speech—*Gespräch* and *Zwiesprache*—between thinker and poet. It would be necessary to meditate on the difference but also the reciprocity (*Wechselbezug*) between the *Erörterung* (the situation, the thought of the site, *Ort*) and the *Erläuterung* (the elucidating reading, the "explication") of a *Gedicht*, the difference between *Gedicht* and *Dichtungen*, etc. Just as I cannot translate these words without lengthy formalities, so for lack of time I will have to restrict myself to this gross affirmation which I think is hardly contestable: statements like those I have just cited and translated by *spirit in-flames* are obviously statements *of* Heidegger. Not his own, productions of the subject Martin Heidegger, but statements to which he subscribes apparently without the slightest reluctance. On the one hand, he opposes them to everything which he is in the process of opposing, and which forms a sufficiently determining context. On the other hand, he supports them in a discourse of which the least one can say is that it does not bear even the trace of a reservation. It would thus be completely irrelevant to reduce these statements in ontological form to "commentaries." Nothing is more foreign to Heidegger than commentary in its ordinary sense—if indeed the word has any other, the concept of which might lay claim to any rigor. Certainly, Heidegger's statements let themselves be *carried, conducted, initiated* here by lines of Trakl's which they seem rather to *precede* or *attract,* guide in their turn. To *set in motion* [*agir*], even. But it is precisely of the coming and going according to this double movement (*ducere/agere*), of this double orientation, that the *Gespräch* speaks. The year, spirit, fire, will be just that, a return of the coming-going. And yet we shall try, *up to a certain point, and provisionally,* to distinguish what is due to [*revient à*] Heidegger. What he says of flame and of spirit certainly lets itself be initiated by the lines in Trakl. Lines which he picks out and chooses in a discreet but extremely active way. Spirit and flame are linked, for example, in the last poem, *Grodek,* which names *"Die heisse Flamme der Geistes,* "the ardent flame of spirit" [179], or the opening of the poem *An Luzifer: "Dem Geist leih deine Flamme, glühende Schwermut,"* "To spirit give up your flame, fervent melancholy" [180].

Given this, the question does not expect to find out who says "spirit-in-flames"—they both say it in their fashion— but to recognize what Heidegger says of *spirit* in order to *situate* such an utterance, both to explain it and to lead it back to its place—if it has a place, and one that is absolutely its own.

Faced with *Geist* this time, with the *Geist* Trakl is talking about, Heidegger is not interested in deconstructing its meaning, or reinscribing it into metaphysics or even Christian theology. On the contrary, he intends to show that Trakl's *Gedicht* (his poetic work if not his poems) has not only crossed the limit of onto-theology: it allows us to think such a crossing [*franchissement*] which is also an enfranchisement [*affranchissement*]. This enfranchisement, still equivocal in Hölderlin, as we have just seen, is *univocal* in Trakl. Never elsewhere did Heidegger attempt to save poetic univocity as he does in a certain passage of this text, which I must be content merely to quote: "Unique of its kind, the rigor of the essentially plurivocal language of Trakl is, in a higher sense, so univocal (*eindeutig*) that it even remains infinitely superior to any technical exactitude of the concept in its simply scientific univocity" (p. 75 [192]).

This *Erörterung* of Trakl's *Gedicht* is, so it seems to me, one of Heidegger's richest texts: subtle, overdetermined, more untranslatable than ever. And, of course, one of the

most problematic. With a violence that I can neither hide
nor assume, I shall have to extract from it the spectrum
[*spectre*] which replies to the names and attributes of spirit
(*Geist, geistig, geistlich*). As I am continuing to study this
text, on the other hand, with a more fitting patience, I hope
one day to be able—beyond what a lecture allows me to do
today—to do justice to it by also analyzing its gesture, its
mode, and its status (if it has one), its relationship with philosophical discourse, with hermeneutics and poetics, but
also what it says of *Geschlecht*, of the word *Geschlecht*, and
also of the place (*Ort*), and of animality. For the moment, I
shall follow only the passage of spirit.

Heidegger seems at first to place his trust in the word
geistlich which he finds in *Verklärter Herbst* (*Transfigured
Autumn*). At the moment of this nonfortuitous encounter
and from the very opening pages, some determining decisions have been taken, already drawing their authority from
the idiom of Old High German [162–63]. In this *Gespräch*,
everything seems to open and let itself be guided by the interpretation of a line from *Frühling der Seele* (*Springtime of
the Soul*):

Es ist die Seele ein Fremdes auf Erden.

Yes, the soul is a stranger upon the earth.

Heidegger immediately disqualifies any "Platonic" hearing
of this. That the soul is a "stranger" does not signify that
one must take it to be imprisoned, exiled, tumbled into the
terrestrial here below, fallen into a body doomed to the corruption (*Verwesen*) of what is lacking in Being and in truth
is not. Heidegger does thus indeed propose a change of
meaning in the interpretation. This change of meaning goes
against Platonism, comes down to an inversion, precisely, of
meaning itself [le sens même], the direction or orientation
of the soul's movement. This reversal of meaning—and of
the meaning of meaning—passes in the first place through

a listening to language. Heidegger first repatriates the word *fremd* from the German language, leading it back to its *"althochdeutsch"* meaning, *fram,* which, he says, "properly means" (*bedeutet eigentlich*): to be on the way towards (*unterwegs nach*) elsewhere and forwards (*anderswohin vorwärts*), with the sense of destination (*Bestimmung*) rather than of wandering. And he concludes from this that, far from being exiled *on the earth* like a fallen stranger, the soul is on the way *towards the earth: Die seele* sucht *die Erde erst, flieht sie nicht,* the soul only *seeks* the earth, it does not flee it (p. 47 [163]). The soul is a stranger because it does not yet inhabit the earth—rather as the word "*fremd*" is strange because its meaning does not yet inhabit, because it no longer inhabits, its proper *althochdeutsch* place.

Given this, by one of those metonymies which are the miracle of this journey, Heidegger assigns to the soul (*ein Fremdes* from *another* poem, *Sebastian im Traum*) the decline called for by a thrush. Then he distinguishes this decline (*Untergang*) from any catastrophe or any erasure in the *Verfall*. Now the word "spiritual" (*geistlich*) belongs to the same stanza as the line "Yes, the soul is on the earth a stranger":

. . . *Geistlich dämmert*
Bläue über dem verhauenen Wald. . . .

It is therefore *geistlich*, spiritually, that the azure blue of the sky becomes crepuscular (*dämmert*). This word, *geistlich*, often returns in Trakl's work. Heidegger announces, then, that it must be an object of meditation. And it will indeed be one of the major threads, if not the most visible, in this interlacing. The azure becomes crepuscular "spiritually," *geistlich*. Now this becoming-crepuscular, this *Dämmerung*, which does not signify a decline (*Untergang*) nor an occidentalization, is of an essential nature (*wesentlichen Wesens*) (p. 47 [164]). And what proves this, according to

Heidegger? Well, *another* poem of Trakl's, entitled, precisely, *Geistliche Dämmerung,* in which the last line speaks of the "spiritual night" (*die geistliche Nacht*). On the basis of this crepuscule or spiritual night is determined the spirituality of the year (*das Geistliche der Jahre*) spoken of in *another* poem, *Unterwegs.* What is the year? The year, *das Jahr,* is a word of Indo-European origin. It apparently recalls the march (*ier, ienai, gehen*), insofar as it translates the race or course of the sun. It is thus this *Gehen,* this going of day or year, morning or evening, sunrise or sunset (*Gehen, Aufgang, Untergang*) which Trakl here determines under the word *das Geistliche.* Crepuscule or night, as *geistlich,* does not signify the negativity of a decline but what shields the year or shelters this course of the sun (ibid.). Spiritual is the gait of the year, the revolutionary coming-going of the very thing which goes (*geht*).

This spiritual journey would permit an interpretation of the decomposition or corruption (*Verwesen*) of the human form spoken of in *Siebengesang des Todes* (*O des Menschen verweste Gestalt*). By that very fact, it also guides the interpretation of this second blow (*Schlag*) which strikes *Geschlecht,* i.e. both the human species and sexual difference. This second blow transforms the simple duality of difference (*Zweifache*) by imprinting agonistic dissension (*Zweitracht*) upon it. It is not here a question of a history of spirit, in the Hegelian or neo-Hegelian sense, but of a spirituality of the year: what *goes* (*geht, gehen, ienai, Jahr*) but goes *returning* rather towards morning, towards the earlier. Let us say—in an indecently hasty formalization—that Heidegger's purpose would, in the end, come down to showing that the morning and night of *this* spirituality are more originary, in Trakl's *Gedicht* thus understood, than the rising and setting of the sun, the Orient and the Occident, the origin and decadence current in the dominant, i.e. metaphysico-Christian interpretation. This morning and this night would be more originary than any onto-theological history, any history and any spirituality apprehended in a metaphysico-Platonic or Christian world.

What then is signified by this supplement of originarity? Does it have the slightest determinable content? That could be one of the forms of the question towards which we are making our way. But also a first sign signaling towards what precedes or exceeds questioning itself.

Geschlecht is fallen (*verfallene*). Its falling would be neither Platonic nor Christian. It is fallen because it has lost its true blow (*den rechten Schlag*). It would thus find itself on the way towards the true blow of this simple difference, towards the softness of this simple duality (*die Sanftmut einer einfältigen Zwiefalt*) in order to deliver duality (*Zwiefache*) from dissension (*Zwietracht*). It is on the way, the way of a return towards this true blow, that the soul follows a stranger (*ein Fremdes*), a foreigner (*Fremdling*).

Who is this stranger? Heidegger follows his steps in Trakl's poem. The stranger, the other (*ener* "in the old language" [pp. 50ff. (165ff.)]), that one (*Jener*), over there, the one from the other bank, is the one who plunges into the night of the spiritual twilight. To do so he leaves, separates himself, says farewell, withdraws, de-ceases. He is *der Abgeschiedene*. This word, in its common use, means the solitary or the dead (the defunct, the deceased). But without here being withdrawn from death, he is above all marked by the separation of the one who goes away toward another sunrise (*Aufgang*). He is the dead man, of course, and the dead man who separates himself insofar as he is also the demented: *der Wahnsinnige*, a word which again Heidegger wants to awaken under its common signification. He recalls that *wana* "means" ohne, "without," and that *Sinnan* "signifies originarily" (*bedeutet ursprünglich*): to travel, to tend towards a place, to take a direction. Sense is always the direction (*sens*) of a road (*sent* and *set* in Indo-European): the stranger, he who is de-ceased, is not simply dead, or mad, he is on the way to an elsewhere. This is what should be understood when Trakl writes: *Der Wahnsinnige ist gestorben* (The madman is dead) or *Man begräbt den Fremden* (The stranger is interred). This stranger, the usual translation would say, is dead, mad and buried. His step carries him into the night, like a *revenant*, towards the more matutinal dawn of what is not yet born, towards the un-born (*das Ungeborene*)—Artaud would perhaps say the *in-nate*.

"*Revenant*" is not a word of Heidegger's, and no doubt he would not like having it imposed on him because of the negative connotations, metaphysical or parapsychic, that he would be at pains to denounce in it. I will not, however, efface it, because of spirit, all the doublings of spirit that still await us, and especially because of what seems to me to call for it in Trakl's text, at least as I would be tempted to read it. But even more, out of fidelity to what, in Heidegger's text, hears the coming and going of this dead man as a coming back [*revenir*] from night to dawn, and finally as the returning [*revenir*] of a spirit. To comprehend this *re-venance* which goes towards a younger morning, to understand that the end of "*verwesenden Geschlechtes*" of the decomposing species *precedes the beginning*, that death comes before birth, and the "later" before the "earlier," it is necessary to arrive, precisely, at a more *originary* essence of time; to return "before" the interpretation of time which has ruled over our representation at least since Aristotle. As end of the *verwesenden Geschlechtes* the end seems to precede the beginning (*Anbeginn*) of the unborn species (*des ungeborenen Geschlechtes*). But this beginning, this more matutinal morning (*die frühere Frühe*) has already sublated, surpassed, in fact overtaken (*überholt*) the end. And the originary essence of time (*das ursprüngliche Wesen der Zeit*) will indeed have been guarded in this archi-origin. If we do not understand how the end seems to precede the beginning, it is because this originary essence is kept beneath a veil. We are still prisoners of the Aristotelian *representation* of time: succession, dimension for a quantitative or qualitative *calculation* of duration. This dimension can let itself be represented either mechanically, or dynamically, or even in relation to the disintegration of the atom (p. 57 [176]).

Once again, after covering a huge amount of ground, it is on the basis of a more originary thinking of time that we will open ourselves to a more appropriate thinking of spirit. For at this point a question imposes itself on Heidegger in the face of all the meanings we have just recognized and displaced, and which all determine the *Abgeschiedenheit* of the Stranger: if the poet says of the dawn, the night, of the stranger's year, of his journeying, his departure, in short, of his de-cease (*Abgeschiedenheit*), that they are *spiritual*, what is then the meaning of this word, *geistlich*?

To listen superficially to him, Heidegger notes, Trakl seems to restrict himself to the common meaning of the word: to its Christian meaning, and even to that of a certain ecclesiastical holiness. Some of Trakl's lines even appear to encourage this interpretation. However, other lines show clearly, according to Heidegger, that the clerical sense is not dominant. The dominant meaning tends rather [*plutôt*] towards the "earlier" [*plus tôt*] of the one who has been dead for a long time. A movement towards that more than matutinal *Frühe*, this more than vernal initiality, the kind which comes even before the first day of spring (*Frühling*), before the principle of the *primum tempus*, comes the day before the day before [*l'avant-veille*]. This *Frühe* as it were keeps vigil for [*veille*] the vernal itself; it is already the promise of the poem *Frühling der Seele* (*Springtime of the Soul*).

The promise must be stressed. The word *versprechen* (to promise) speaks the singular *Frühe* promised (*verspricht*) by a poem entitled *Frühling der Seele*. But we also find it again near the conclusion, when Heidegger is speaking of the West (*Abendland* and *Abendländisches Lied* are the titles of two other poems). Referring to the poem entitled *Herbstseele* (*Autumn Soul*), he distinguishes between the West which Trakl gives us to think and that of Platonic-Christian Europe. He writes of this West what is also valid for the archior pre-oriental *Frühe*—and again emphasizes the promise: "This West is older, i.e. *früher*, more precocious [more initial, but no word fits here] and thereby promising more (*versprechender*) than the Platonic-Christian West and, quite simply, more than the one we imagine in the European fashion.³

Versprechender: promising more not because it would be more promising, because it would promise more, more things, but promising better, more apt [*propre*] for the promise, closer to the essence of an authentic promise.

This promise poses nothing, pro-mises nothing, it does not put forward, it speaks. One could say that this *Sprache verspricht*, and I would say (Heidegger does not say it like this) that it is in the opening of this *Sprache* that the speaking of the *Dichter* and that of the *Denker* cross in their *Gespräch* or their *Zwiesprache*. Naturally the promise of this *Versprechen* can be corrupted, dissimulated, or can go astray. It is even this affliction of the promise that Heidegger is meditating here when he speaks of the European Platonic-Christian West and the *Verwesen* of humanity or, rather, of *Geschlecht*. This *Verwesen* is also a corruption of the *Versprechen*, a fatal corruption which does not befall *Sprache* as an accident.

In another context,⁴ pretending to play without playing with Heidegger's famous formula (*Die Sprache spricht*), Paul de Man wrote: *Die Sprache verspricht.* He was not playing, the game is at work in language itself. One day he sharpened up this formula as *Die Sprache verspricht sich:* language or speech promises, promises *itself* but also goes back on its word, becomes undone or unhinged, derails or becomes delirious, deteriorates, becomes corrupt just as immediately and just as essentially. It cannot not promise as soon as it speaks, it is promise, but it cannot fail to break its promise—and this comes of the structure of the promise, as of the event it nonetheless institutes. The *Verwesen* is a *Versprechen*. In saying this, I have perhaps, doubtless even (how could one be sure?) left the order of commentary, if such a thing exists. Would Heidegger subscribe to an interpretation which would make of this *Versprechen* something other than a modality or modification of *Sprache*? He would, rather [*plutôt*], earlier [*plus tôt*], see the very coming, in the promise, for better and for worse, of the *given word*. It remains to find out whether this *Versprechen* is not the promise which, opening every speaking, makes possible the very question and therefore precedes it without belonging to it: the dissymmetry of an affirmation, of a *yes* before all opposition of *yes* and *no*. The call of Being—every question already responds to it, the promise has already taken place wherever language comes. Language always, *before any question*,[5] and in the very question, comes down to [*revient à*] the promise. This would also be a promise *of spirit*.

By promising better, by according itself with what is most essentially promise in the best promise, what is *versprechender* thus announces the day before the day before: what has already taken place, in some sense, even before what we, in our Europe, call the origin or the first day of spring [*le premier temps du printemps*]. That a promise announce or salute what has taken place "before" the *previously*—that is the style of temporality or historiality, that is a coming of the event, *Ereignis* or *Geschehen*, which we must think in order to approach the spiritual, the *Geistliche* hidden under the Christian or Platonic representation. The "must" of this "we must think" in truth accords its modality to that of the promise. Thought is fidelity to this promise. Which means that it is only what it should be if it listens—if it both hears and obeys.

We have just seen why this use of the word *geistlich*

ought not to be Christian. And why, despite so many appearances, Trakl or at least Trakl's *Gedicht ought* not to be essentially Christian. Heidegger here inscribes invisible quotation marks in the use of the *same* word. This word is thus divided by an internal difference. As for the adjective *geistig*, which, as we saw, he used extensively without quotation marks and took for his own, continually from 1933, now he brutally sends it packing, without more ado. With what can look like a flagrant lack of consistency, he behaves as though he had not been celebrating the *Geistigkeit* of *Geist* for twenty years. This word, in the name of which, and from what a height, he had denounced all the forms of "destitution of spirit," he now inscribes in the massive and crudely typecast form of the metaphysico-Platonic tradition, the tradition responsible for or symptomatic of this *Verwesen* of *Geschlecht*: the corruption of the human race in its sexual difference. Here he is now *recognizing* the whole of Platonism in this word. It is better to quote here the passage in which reappears the *vermeiden*, the gesture of avoiding, which I mentioned at the start. It resounds here like a delayed echo of the same word in *Sein und Zeit*, a quarter of a century earlier. But an abyss henceforth amplifies the resonance. Heidegger has just noted that *geistlich* does not have the Christian sense. He then pretends to wonder why Trakl said *geistliche* and not *geistige Dämmerung* or *geistige Nacht*. Here is the passage:

> Why, then, does he avoid (*vermeidet er*) the word "*geistig*"? Because "*Geistige*" names the contrary opposed to the material (*Stofflichen*). This contrary represents (*stellt . . . vor*) the difference between two domains and, in a Platonic-Occidental language, names the abyss (*Kluft*) between the suprasensible (*noeton*) and the sensible (*aistheton*).
>
> The spiritual thus understood (*Das so verstandene Geistige*) which has meanwhile become the rational, the intellectual and the ideological, belongs with its

oppositions to the apprehension of the world (*Weltansicht*) of the "*verwesenden Geschlecht*," of *Geschlecht* in decomposition. (p. 59 [178–79])

The degradation of the spiritual into the "rational," "intellectual," "ideological" is indeed what Heidegger was condemning in 1935. From this point of view the continuity of his remarks appears incontestable. But, in 1935, he was speaking in the name of *Geistigkeit* and not of *Geistlichkeit*, especially not of that (non-Christian) *Geistlichkeit*. He was speaking in the name of what he has just defined as the Platonic origin of the misinterpretation and degradation of spirit. At least he was doing so *literally*, since he constantly made use of the word "*geistig*," but the distinction between the letter and something else (for example the spirit) has precisely no pertinence here other than a Platonic-Christian one.

Those are, then, *negative* approaches to the essence of spirit. In its most proper essence, as the poet and thinker allow it to be approached, *Geist is neither* Christian *Geistlichkeit nor* Platonic-metaphysical *Geistigkeit*.

What is it, then? What is *Geist*? In order to reply to this question in an affirmative mode, still listening to Trakl, Heidegger invokes the flame.

Spirit *in-flames:* how to hear or understand this?

It is not a figure, not a metaphor. Heidegger, at least, would contest any rhetoricizing reading.[6] One could attempt to bring the concepts of rhetoric to bear here only after making sure of some proper meaning for one or other of these words, spirit, flame, in such and such a determinate language, in such and such a text, in such and such a sentence. We are far from that and everything comes back to this difficulty.

Not being able to follow Heidegger here step by step, I shall simply mark out the reading I should like to propose with a few *traits*. Why *traits*? Because the motif of the trait

will, so to speak, make an incision within the flame. And
the trait will be something quite different from what we
mean in French by *trait d'esprit.*
1. *First trait.* Heidegger does not simply reject the determination of spirit as *spiritus* and *pneuma,* in the passage I
am going to quote. Rather, he derives it, he affirms the de-
pendence of breath, wind, respiration, inspiration, expira-
tion, and sighing in regard to flame. It is because *Geist* is
flame that there is *pneuma* and *spiritus.* But spirit is not
first, not originarily *pneuma* or *spiritus.*
2. *Second trait.* In this movement, the recourse to the
German language appears irreducible. It appears to make the
semantics of *Geist* depend on an "originary meaning" (*ursprüngliche Bedeutung*) entrusted to the German idiom
gheis.
3. *Third trait.* In the affirmative determination of spirit—
spirit in-flames—the internal possibility of the worst is already lodged. Evil has its provenance in spirit itself. It is born
of spirit but, precisely, of a spirit which is not the
metaphysico-Platonic *Geistigkeit.* Evil is not on the side of
matter or of the sensible matter generally opposed to spirit.
Evil is spiritual, it is also *Geist,* whence this other internal
duplicity which makes one spirit into the evil ghost of the
other. In the passage I am going to quote, this duplicity affects all the thinking up to and including that of ash, that
whiteness of ash which belongs to destiny consumed and
consuming, to the conflagration of the flame which burns
itself up. Is ash the Good or the Evil of flame?
   I first translate a few lines before picking out some other
traits:

> But what is spirit? In his last poem, *Grodek,* Trakl
> speaks of the "burning flame of spirit" (*heissen
> Flamme des Geistes*) (201). Spirit is what flares up (*das
> Flammende:* spirit in flames) and it is perhaps only as
> such that it blows (that it is a breath, *ein Wehendes*).
> Trakl does not understand spirit primarily as *pneuma,*

not spiritually (*nicht spirituell:* a very rare occurrence of this word in Heidegger), but as the flame which flames [or inflames itself, *entflammt:* what is proper to spirit is this auto-affective spontaneity which has need of no exteriority to catch fire or set fire, to pass ecstatically outside itself; it gives itself Being outside itself, as we shall see: spirit in flames—gives and catches fire all by itself, for better and for worse, since it also affects itself with evil and is the passage outside itself], it raises (or hunts out, *aufjagt*), it displaces [or deposes or frightens, transports or transposes, deports: *entsetzt,* one word, a whole semantics which plays an important role in this text and will soon reappear in the etymological derivation of "*Geist*"], it takes out of reach (*ausser Fassung bringt*). The burning up is the radiance of a reddening glare. What burns itself up is Being-outside-itself (*das Ausser-sich*) which illuminates and makes shine, which also, however (*indessen auch*), can devour tirelessly and consume everything up to and including the white of the ash (*in das Weisse der Asche verzehren kann*).

"The flame is the brother of the palest" is what we read in the poem *Verwandlung des Bösen* (129) (*Transmutation of the Evil One*). Trakl envisages "spirit" on the basis of this essence which is named in the originary meaning (*in der ursprünglichen Bedeutung*) of the word "*Geist,*" for *gheis* means: to be thrown (*aufgebracht*), transported [or transposed, deported: *entsetzt,* again—and I believe this is the most determining predicate], outside itself (*ausser sich*). (pp. 59–60 [179])

X

This is neither the place nor the time—it is too late—to reawaken the wars of etymology, nor, though I am so often tempted to do so, all the ghosts flapping in the wings of this "alchemical theater," as Artaud would say. And one of the most obsessing ghosts among the philosophers of this alchemy would again be Hegel who, as I have tried to show elsewhere,[1] situated the passage from the philosophy of nature to the philosophy of spirit in the combustion from which, like the sublime effluvia of a fermentation, *Geist*—the gas—rises up or rises up again above the decomposing dead, to interiorize itself in the *Aufhebung*.

Let us then leave etymology and ghosts—but is it not the same question?—and keep ourselves provisionally to the internal logic of this discourse, or more precisely, to the way in which this interiority, or rather this *familial* internalization, is constituted: this domestication in a place where the thought about spirit appears at its most idiomatic, when the flame of *Geist*, for better or for worse, burns in the hearth of one language only. I said something about it just now, when I marked the double dissymmetry determining the Graeco-German couple. What has just been clarified on this subject? Apparently, we have a trio of languages: Greek (*pneuma*), Latin (*spiritus*), German (*Geist*). Heidegger does not disqualify the immense semantics of breathing, of inspiration or respiration, imprinted in Greek or Latin. He simply says they are less originary.[2] But this supplement of originary status he assigns to German only has meaning, and can only be said, inside a triangle or a linguistico-historical triad, and only if one grants a sort of *history of the meaning* of the "thing" *pneuma-spiritus-Geist* which is both European and, by means of *Geist* interpreted in this way, has a bearing beyond or before Western Europe in its usual representation.

To someone who reproached him with not caring about other languages, what could Heidegger say? First of all this, perhaps: what he thinks in his language—and one does not think outside a language—is held in this intra-translational triangle. He would say that *Geist* does have a more originary sense than *pneuma* and *spiritus,* but historially it is held in a relationship of translation such that the German thinker inhabits *this* space, and only in this triangular place *outside which* one can certainly encounter all kinds of meanings of at least equal worth, themselves calling forth tempting analogies, but for which translation as *pneuma, spiritus,* or *Geist* would demonstrate a levity abusive and ultimately violent for the languages thereby assimilated.

I would not dispute the very strong "logic" of this response if the historial triangle could legitimately be closed. In fact, it seems that it is closed only by an act of brutal foreclosure. "Foreclosure" figures a word common in various codes (law, psychoanalysis) to say too rapidly and too firmly something of this *avoiding* which we are cautiously trying to think through here. Such a "foreclosure," then, seems certainly significant in itself, in its content, but what interests me here is simply its value as a symptom, as it were, and to maintain a question of principle: what justifies the closure of this triangle "historially"? Does it not remain open from its origin and by its very structure onto what Greek and then Latin *had* to translate by *pneuma* and *spiritus,* that is, the Hebrew *ruah*?

A clarification, first, as to the ultimate dimensions of this question; it concerns less a *historial* avoiding, as I have just overhastily suggested, than the very determination of a historiality in general from the limits which such an avoiding would come along to set. What Heidegger names *Geschichte*, and all the meanings he associates with this, would be deployed in the advent and as the very instituting of this triangle.

Without being able to invoke here the vast corpus of prophetic texts and their translations, without doing any more than recalling what makes it permissible to read a whole tradition of Jewish thought as an inexhaustible thinking about *fire*;[3] without citing the evidence from the Gospels of a pneumatology which has an ineradicable relationship of translation with *ruah*, I will refer only to one distinction, made by Paul in the First Epistle to the Corinthians (2:14), between *pneuma* and *psyche*. Corresponding to the distinction between *ruah* and *néphéch*, it belongs—if it is not its opening—to the theologico-philosophical tradition in which Heidegger continues to interpret the relationship between *Geist* and *Seele*.[4]

Once this immense problem has been pointed out, can one not wonder about the legitimacy of the historial closure of speech in which Heidegger repeats and claims to go beyond the European race from East to West? Leaving aside the fact that, among other traits, for example those that sometimes make it a "holy spirit" (*ruah haqqodech, ruah qodech*), the *ruah* can also, like *Geist*, carry evil within it. It can become *ruah raa*, the evil spirit. Heidegger delimits not only this or that misinterpretation of *Geistigkeit* in the name of an authentic *Geistigkeit*, as he did in 1933–35, but also the whole European and Christian-metaphysical discourse which holds to the word *geistig* instead of thinking the *geistliche* in the sense supposedly given it by Trakl. Given this, it is his own strategy of 1935, entirely dominated by a still limited use of the word *geistig*, which is targeted, comprehended, compromised, and even deconstructed by this new delimitation.

Now this is the moment at which Heidegger violently closes or encloses the European in idioms which had, however, *incorporated* the translation of at least one language and of a historiality which is here never named, never thought, and which perhaps would no longer submit to historial epochality and to the history of Being. What, then, would be the most appropriate place for the questions we are pointing to here? Perhaps that which Heidegger himself situates beyond history or the epochality of Being: a certain thinking of *Ereignis*.

The allusion to the *ruah raa*, to the evil spirit, leads me towards another of the traits which I must underline. Spirit—in flames—deploys its essence (*west*), says Heidegger, according to the possibility of gentleness (*des Sanften*) *and* of destruction (*des Zerstörerischen*). The white of ash, one could say, here figures that destruction according to radical evil. Evil and wickedness are spiritual (*geistlich*) and not simply sensible or material, by simple metaphysical opposition to that which is *geistig*. Heidegger insists on this with formulas which are sometimes literally Schellingian, in the wake of the 1809 *Treatise on the Essence of Human Freedom* and the course Heidegger devoted to it in 1936. Why can this continuity appear both natural and troubling? Because the "Schellingian" formulas which sustain this interpretation of Trakl seem to belong, following Heidegger's own course, to that metaphysics of evil and the will which at the time he was trying to delimit rather than accept. What is more, Heidegger also tried, in 1936, to withdraw this Schellingian thinking of evil, however metaphysical it still was (or because it had the authenticity of a great metaphysics) from a purely Christian space.[5] But the distinctions can never be so simple in the tangled topology of these displacements. Some of the formulas of the essay on Trakl recall the course on Schelling precisely in this gesture towards going, so to speak, beyond Christianity. But the same formulas confirm a metaphysics of evil, a metaphysics of the will, thus also that metaphysics of *humanitas* and *animalitas* which we have recognized in the teaching of the same period (*In-*

troduction to Metaphysics, 1935) and which Heidegger, so it seems to me, never went back on.[6] Here is one among so many other possible examples, and I choose it for reasons of *proximity*. Heidegger writes of the *Metamorphosis of the Evil One*, immediately after evoking the "original signification" of the word *Geist*:

> Thus understood, spirit deploys its essence (*west*) in the possibility of gentleness and destruction. Gentleness does not submit to some repression (*schlägt keineswegs nieder*) the being-outside-itself of conflagration (*des Entflammenden*), but holds it gathered (*versammelt*) in the peace of friendship. Destruction comes from the frenzy which consumes (*verzehrt*) itself on its own insurrection and in this way pushes the evil one (*das Bösartige betreibt*). Evil is always the evil of a spirit. Evil, and its malignity, is not the sensible, the material. No more is it of a simply "spiritual" nature (*"geistiger" Natur*). Evil is spiritual (*geistlich*) [. . .]. (p. 60 [179])

Now in his *Schelling* he wrote:

> an animal can never be "wicked," even if we sometimes express ourselves in these terms. For to wickedness belongs spirit (*Denn zur Bosheit gehört Geist*). The animal can never leave the unity proper to the determined place in nature which is its own. Even when an animal is "cunning," "malicious," this malice remains limited to a quite determined field, and when it manifests itself, this is always in circumstances equally very determined; and then it comes into play automatically. Man, on the contrary, is that being who can overturn the elements which compose his essence, overturn the ontological fit (*die Seynsfuge*) of his *Dasein* and disjoin it (*ins Ungefüge*). [. . .] It is therefore to man that is reserved the dubious privilege of being able to fall lower than the animal, while the animal is not capable of this mal-version (*Verkehrung*) of prin-

ciples. [. . .] The ground of evil thus resides in the primordial will (*Urwillen*) of the primary base. (pp. 173–74 [p. 146])

Let us finally situate a last *trait*, the *trait itself, Riss.* This word also traces difference. It returns often to bespeak the retreat by which spirit relates to itself and divides in that sort of internal adversity which gives rise to evil, by inscribing it, as it were, right in the flame. Like fire-writing. This is not an accident. It does not befall, after the event and as an extra, the flame of light. Flame writes, writes itself, right in the flame. Trait of conflagration, spirit in-flames—traces the route, breaks the path:

> To the extent that the essence of spirit resides in conflagration (*in Entflammen*), it breaks the path (*bricht er Bahn*), makes its clearing and sets it on the road. As flame, spirit is the tempest (*Sturm*) which "storms the sky" ("*den Himmel stürmt*") and gives itself over to "ousting God" ("*Gott erjagt*"). Spirit pursues (*jagt*) the soul on the way (*in das Unterwegs*). . . . (*Unterwegs zur Sprache*, p. 60 [179–80])

The path-breaking [*frayage*] of this trait (trace, attraction, contraction) thus, and first of all, brings spirit back to soul. Spirit throws and pursues soul on the way, in the way opened by its fire, and this is the being-on-the-way (*Unterwegs*) of migration but also of overtaking, of precipitation or anticipation (*wo sich ein Vorauswandern begibt*) according to that temporality which makes the end appear before the beginning. It is thus that spirit transposes, deposes, and deports into the foreign (*versetzt in das Fremde*), it transports the soul. Thus, again, "*Es ist die Seele ein Fremdes auf Erden.*" This deportation is a gift. "The spirit is what makes a gift of soul" (*Der Geist ist es, der mit Seele beschenkt*). This is why it is also, in a still Hölderlinian formulation, the *Beseeler.*" Conversely, the soul guards (*hütet*) spirit, "nourishes" it, and this in so essential a fashion that we may presume, Heidegger adds, that there would be no spirit without soul. *Guard* and *nourishment* would again stress, in the sense of a tradition, the femininity of the soul, here indissociably coupled—and we will not invoke the grammar of genders—with a masculine spirit which draws on, hunts, chases, sends on the way, and marks with its trait—and, what is more, a trait of flame.[7]

Solitary and voyaging, the soul must assume the weight of its destiny (*Geschick*). It must gather itself in the One, carry and carry itself towards the essence assigned to it, migration—but not wandering. It must carry itself *before*, to encounter spirit (*dem Geist entgegen*). Fervor of *Gemüt*, flame or ardent melancholy, the soul must consent, or lend itself, to spirit:

Dem Geist leih deine Flamme, glühende Schwermut

The soul is *great* according to the measure of this flame and of its sadness:

O Schmerz, du flammendes Anschaun
Der Grossen Seele!
(Das Gewitter [183])

This is the *trait*, the division or adversity even inside sadness, for sadness has in itself, proper to itself, an essence of adversity (*Dem Schmerz eignet ein in sich gegenwendiges Wesen*). It is in the mark (*Riss*) of the flame that sadness carries away, tears apart, or snatches at the soul.

"'Flammend' reisst der Schmerz fort," Heidegger says in his commentary on *Das Gewitter*, "The Storm." *Sein Fortriss zeichnet die wandernde Seele in die Fuge des Stürmens und Jagens ein*. . . . It is difficult to translate. As often, I paraphrase instead—and the word *Fuge* is more resistant than others: the dominant mark inscribes the voyaging soul in adjustment, the just according of the storm and the pursuit which, mounting to the assault of the sky (*den Himmel stürmend*), would like to deliver itself to ousting God (*Gott erjagen möchte).* Across all these modifications (*Riss, Fort-riss, Rückniss,* but also *Zug, Bezug, Grundzug, ziehen),* the trait or the re-trait of what *has trait* [*a trait*] inscribes evil. The trait engraves sadness in the essence of *spirit's relation to itself* which gathers and divides itself in this way. It is in sadness that spirit gives the soul. Which in turn bears the spirit. In the soul, then, rules the fundamental trait (*Grund-zug*) of sadness. It is its essence. And it is the essence of the Good. By the same fundamental trait, the Good is the Good only in sadness. Sadness carries off [*emporte*] (*fortreisst),* and properly (*eigentlich*), in the re-trait of its tearing trait (*als zurückreissender Riss*).

A doubly remarkable trait. Redoubled, itself a double mark, and right on the spirit, it is the spirit in which it in-scribes itself, traces itself, retires, or retracts. It belongs to the flame it divides. And it has an essential affinity with the blow, the strike, the imprint (*Schlag),* from which Heidegger, in his language, interprets *Geschlecht,* in its just striking and then in the bad blow which deposes or corrupts it into *verwesende Geschlecht* whose duality is dedicated to dis-sension (*Zwietracht).* The blow, the just but also the bad one, the second, the wound, the malediction (these are Hei-degger's words) which strike the human *Geschlecht,* are blows of spirit. The vocabulary often still appears Schellin-gian.[8] Just one quotation: "But who has guard over this pow-erful sadness for it to nourish the burning flame of spirit? That which bears the impress of the spirit (*Was vom Schlage dieses Geistes ist*) belongs to that which sets on the way. That which bears the impress of this spirit is called *geist-lich.*"

On the other hand, the difference or duality inscribed by the trait or even by the impress is not considered by Heideg-ger as a *division.* It is the relation of spirit itself to itself as *gathering together.* The trait gathers. The word *Ver-sammlung* (gathering) traverses, dominates, and overdeter-mines this whole meditation. It gathers all that is gathering:

the place (*Ort*), the de-cease (*Abgeschiedenheit*), the soul which solitude carries toward the "unique" and gathers in the One (*in das Eine*) (p. 61 [180]), the *Gemüt*, and finally the one itself (*Ein*) of *Ein Geschlecht*, that One which is, apparently, the only word italicized in Trakl's work. This One is not, Heidegger says, identity, indifference, or sexual uniformity, but the most matutinal morning to which the stranger's march will have destined him. Now the *Versammlung*, this gathering in the One, is also called *Geist* by Heidegger, and he does so in formulations which here again often recall Schelling. The separation of what takes its departure in de-cease is none other, in its very burning up, than spirit, "*der Geist und als dieser das Versammelnde*": spirit and, as such, what gathers (p. 66 [185]).

It is too late and I won't keep you here until morning.

Schematizing to the extreme, one can perhaps see two paths of thought here crossing under Heidegger's step. And without criticizing, without even asking questions in pretense of conclusion, I shall hold, in the very dry description of these two paths, only to what can still say something to us—at least I imagine it can—about *our* steps, and about a certain crossing of *our* paths. About a *we* which is perhaps not *given*.

One of the paths—its trail can be followed in the reading of Trakl—would lead back to the spirituality of a promise which, without being opposed to Christianity, would be foreign to it, and even at the origin of Christianity (to which we can give several names), still more radically foreign to Platonic metaphysics and all that follows from it, foreign to a certain European determination of the course from East to West. What is most matutinal in the *Frühe*, in its best promise, would in truth be of an *other* birth and an *other* essence, origin-heterogeneous [*hétérogène à l'origine*] to all the testaments, all the promises, all the events, all the laws and assignments which are our very memory. *Origin-heterogeneous*: this is to be understood at once, all at once, in three senses: (1) heterogeneous from the origin, originarily heterogeneous; (2) heterogeneous with respect to what is called the origin, other than the origin and irreducible to it; (3) heterogeneous *and* or *insofar as* at the origin, origin-heterogeneous because at the origin of the origin. Heterogeneous *because* it is and *although* it is at the origin. *"Because"* and *"although" at the same time*, that's the logical form of the tension which makes all this thinking hum. The circle which, via death, decline, the West, returns towards the most originary, that towards which we are called by the *Gespräch* between Heidegger and Trakl, would be quite other than the analogous circles or revolutions the thinking of which we have inherited, from what are called the Testaments up to and including Hegel or Marx, not to mention some other modern thinkers. Given this, these words: "circle, decline, West" would be paleonyms. They deserve only the quotation marks necessary to suspend them in a writing or reading which must carry us beyond. I would be tempted to say of this trail that on the one hand it seems to promise, hail, or save *more* or *better*, since it makes appeal to something quite different. An announcement which is more provocative, disturbing, irruptive. But on the other hand, at least as to what puts it to the test in the reading of Trakl, this trail appears to be scarcely passable, even as the impassable itself. Right down into the detail of what I shall dare to call the *explication de texte*, or at any rate the elucidation (*Erläuterung*, which Heidegger distinguishes from the *Erörterung*), the gestures made to snatch Trakl away from the Christian thinking of *Geist* seem to me laborious, violent, sometimes simply caricatural, and all in all not very convincing. I shall try to explain what I mean elsewhere. It is with reference to an extremely conventional and doxical outline of Christianity that Heidegger can claim to de-Christianize Trakl's *Gedicht*. What is *origin-heterogeneous* would in that case be nothing other—but it's not nothing—

than the origin of Christianity: the spirit of Christianity or the essence of Christianity.

One can, then, imagine a scene between Heidegger and certain Christian theologians, perhaps the most demanding, most patient, most impatient. In its program or its type, this meeting has not, moreover, failed to occur. In any case its "logic" seems prescribed. It would in truth be an odd *exchange*. Let us understand by that that the places can sometimes be exchanged in a disturbing way. And as, since the beginning of this lecture, we have been speaking of nothing but the "translation" of these thoughts and discourses into what are commonly called the "events" of "history" and of "politics" (I place quotation marks around all these obscure words), it would also be necessary to "translate" what such an exchange of places can imply in its most radical possibility. This "translation" appears to be both indispensable and for the moment impossible. It therefore calls for quite other protocols, those in view of which I have proposed this reading. What I am aiming at here is, obviously enough, anything but abstract. We are talking about past, present, and future "events," a composition of forces and discourses which seem to have been waging merciless war on each other (for example from 1933 to our time). We have here a program and a combinatory whose power remains abyssal. In all rigor it exculpates none of the discourses which can thus exchange their power. It leaves no place open for any arbitrating authority. Nazism was not born in the desert. We all know this, but it has to be constantly recalled. And even if, far from any desert, it had grown like a mushroom in the silence of a European forest, it would have done so in the shadow of big trees, in the shelter of their silence or their indifference but in the same soil. I will not list these trees which in Europe people an immense black forest, I will not count the species. For essential reasons, the presentation of them defies tabular layout. In their bushy taxonomy, they would bear the names of religions, philosophies, political regimes, economic structures, religious or academic institutions. In short, what is just as confusedly called culture, or the world of spirit.

The first, then, those I called theologians and all those they might represent, would say to Heidegger: "But what you call the archi-originary spirit, which you claim is foreign to Christianity, is indeed what is most essential in Christianity. Like you, it's what we would like to revive under the theologemes, philosophemes, or common representations. We give thanks for what you say, you have a right to all our gratitude [reconnaissance] for what you give us to hear and think—and which we do indeed recognize [reconnaissons]. It's precisely what we have always been seeking. And when you speak of promise, this *Versprechen*, of a more than matutinal dawn beyond a beginning and an end of history, before and beyond East and West, do you realize just how close to us you are? And even more so when you speak of fall (*Verfall*) and malediction (*Fluch*). And even more so when you speak of spiritual evil. And even more so when, in the trace of this line from Trakl,

Gott sprach eine sanfte Flamme zu seinem Herzen:
O Mensch!

you name this word of God, his *Sprechen*—which we are tempted to link with the *Versprechen* just mentioned—when you accord it with a *Zusprechen* or a *Zuspruch* (instruction [*mandement*], consolation, exhortation) (p. 79 [196]), which calls us to the *Entsprechung*, to correspondence. And even more so when you speak of a resurrection to come of the *Menschenschlag* from the dawn (*in ein kommendes Auferstehen des Menschenschlages aus der Frühe* (p. 67 [185]) or of salvation and the blow which saves (*rettet*); and when, making clear above all that this mission or this sending of the blow struck (*das Geschick des Schlages*) strikes with difference (specifies by separating: *verschlägt*) the *Menschengeschlecht*, i.e. saves it (*d.h. rettet*) (p. 80 [195]), you say that this 'i.e.,' this joining of blow and salvation in an archi-originary and yet-to-come event, is a hymn—let's say a hymn of praise—which the poet sings, and not stories which historians tell. When you say all that, we who would like to be authentic Christians think that you are going to the essence of what we want to think, revive, restore, in our faith, and even if we have to do it against these common representations with which you wish at all costs to confuse Christianity (which elsewhere you know so well), against certain theologemes or certain onto-theological philosophemes. You say the most radical things that can be said when one is a Christian today. At this point, especially when you speak of God, of *retrait*, of flame and fire-writing in the promise, in accord with the promise of return towards the land of pre-archi-originarity, it is not certain that you would not receive a comparable reply and similar echo from my friend and coreligionary, the Messianic Jew. I'm not certain that the Moslem and some others wouldn't join in the concert or the hymn. At least all those who in religions and philosophies have spoken of *ruah*, *pneuma*, *spiritus* and, why not, *Geist*."

Since I'm doing the questions and answers here, I imagine Heidegger's reply. We can reconstruct it on the basis of the program of typical strategies which he has, after all, bequeathed to us: "But in affirming that Trakl's *Gedicht*—and everything I say along with it—is neither metaphysical nor Christian, I am opposing nothing, especially not Christianity, nor all the discourses of the fall, of malediction, of the promise, of salvation, of resurrection, nor the discourses on *pneuma* and *spiritus*, nor even (I'd forgotten that one) on *ruah*. I'm simply trying, modestly, discreetly, to think that *on the basis of which* all this is possible. That (on the basis of which. . . .), because it has always been veiled, *is not yet what it makes possible*. That 'on the basis of which,' that more than originary *Frühe*, is not yet thinkable, it remains to come. A circle draws this *Frühe* from the day before the day before up to that morning which has not yet come, and this circle is not—not yet or already no more—the circle of European metaphysics, or the eschatologies, the messianisms or apocalypses of all sorts. I did not say that the flame was *something other or opposite* then pneumatological or spiritual breathing, I said that it is on the basis of flame that one thinks *pneuma* and *spiritus* or, since you insist, *ruah,* etc. I simply said, *Geist* is not *first of all* this, that, or the other."

This retreat [*retraite*] of Heidegger's, of which we have the regular, typical, and recurrent signs in his text, is one of the two paths in the crossing I mentioned a moment ago and which further runs the risk—crossing is not a neutral word—of recalling the cross-shaped crossing-through under which one leaves Being or God to suffer.[9] Heidegger's *retrait,* in this crossing, would be one of the two steps, or rather [*plutôt*] the step toward the "earlier" [*le "plus tôt"*]. It leads to making this powerful thinking repetition into a *retrait* or an advance towards the most originary, the pre-archi-originary which only thinks *more* [*qui ne pense* plus]—and thus better—by thinking *nothing more* [*rien . . . de plus*], nothing other in any case, no other content than what is there, even as the promise of the future, in the legacy of metaphysics or the traditions—let's say religious ones—and, more generally, in this world of which, in 1935, Heidegger said it is always a spiritual world. But if one made of this an objection or reproach against Heidegger, if one said to him that this repetition adds, invents or discovers nothing, that it merely redoubles hollowly, by an experience which is, all in all, that of truth as memory and memory as promise, the event of a promise which has already taken place, Heidegger, I imagine, would reply: "in what you call the path of repetition which adds nothing (but what do you want to add? Do you find that what we have in our memory, the abyss of our memory, is not enough?), the thinking of this *Frühe* to come, while advancing towards the possibility of what you think you recognize, is going towards what is quite other than what you think you recognize. It is indeed not a new content. But access to thought, the thinking access to the *possibility* of metaphysics or pneumato-spiritualist religions opens onto something quite other than what the possibility makes possible. It opens onto what remains *origin-heterogeneous.* What you represent as a simply ontological and transcendental replica is quite other. This is why, without opposing myself to that of which I am trying to think the most matutinal possibility, without even using words other than those of the tradition, I follow the path of a repetition which crosses the path of the entirely other. The entirely other announces itself in the most rigorous repetition. And this repetition is also the most vertiginous and the most abyssal."

"Yes, precisely," his interlocutors would then reply, "that's just what we're saying, at the same crossing of paths, and these paths would be equally but otherwise circular: we are appealing to this entirely other in the memory of a promise or the promise of a memory. That's the truth of what we have always said, heard, tried to make heard. The misunderstanding is that you hear us better than you think or pretend to think. In any case, no misunderstanding on our part, from now on, it's enough to keep talking, not to interrupt—between the poet and you, which means just as much between you and us—this *Zwiesprache.* It's enough not to interrupt the colloquium, even when it is already late. The spirit which keeps watch in returning [*en revenant,* as a ghost] will always do the rest. Through flame or ash, but as the entirely other, inevitably."

NOTES

(Unless otherwise indicated, all notes are the author's.)

CHAPTER I

1. This is the title of a chapter in a book published simultaneously with the present work: *Psyché. Inventions de l'autre*
(Paris: Galilée, 1987), pp. 535–95. See too, in the same book, "Désistance," pp. 597–638.

2. Reply to students at the University of Zurich (1951). Seminar
translated and presented by F. Fédier and D. Saatdjian in the journal
Po∂sie 13 (1980). The passage I quote and to which I return in
"Comment ne pas parler" (in *Psyché*) was also translated in the
same year by J. Greisch in *Heidegger et la question de Dieu* (Paris:
Grasset, 1980), p. 334.

3. "Within thought, nothing can be accomplished which could
prepare or contribute to the determination of what happens in faith
and grace. If faith were to call me in this way, I should shut up shop.
Of course, within the dimension of faith, one still continues thinking; but thought as such no longer has any task to fulfil." Report of
a session of the Evangelical Academy in Hofgeismar, December
1953, translated by J. Greisch in *Heidegger et la question de Dieu*,
p. 335.

4. Since the whole of this discourse will be surrounded by fire, I
recall briefly that Helvétius's book *De l'esprit* was burned at the
foot of the great staircase of the Palais de Justice on 10 February
1759 by order of the Parlement of Paris, after the king had withdrawn its *privilège* and Pope Clement XIII had forbidden it to be
read *in any language*. The author's second, more or less sincere,
retraction is well known: I quote from it a few lines which are not

without their bearing, although extremely indirect, on what we are dealing with here: "I did not want to attack either the nature of the soul, or its origin, or its spirituality, as I thought I had made clear at several points in this work: I did not want to attack any of the truths of Christianity, which I profess sincerely in all the rigor of its dogma and morality, and to which I take pride in submitting all my thoughts, all my opinions, and all the faculties of my being, in the certainty that anything which does not conform to its spirit cannot conform to the truth."

As is also well known, Rousseau agreed neither with Helvétius nor with his persecutors. Fire again: "A few years ago, on the appearance of a famous book (De l'esprit), I resolved to attack its principles, which I found dangerous. I was carrying out this undertaking when I learned that the author was being prosecuted. Immediately I threw my papers into the fire, judging that no duty could authorize the baseness involved in joining with the crowd to crush a man of honor in oppression. When everything had calmed down, I had the opportunity to air my feelings about the same subject in other writings; but I did so without naming the book or its author" (Lettres de la Montagne, 1764 [in Oeuvres complétes, 4 vols (Paris: Gallimard, 1959–69), vol 3. p. 693]).

From spirit—to fire [de l'esprit—au feu]: since this could be the subtitle of this note, let us address a thought to the heretics of the Libre Esprit. The author of the Mirouer des simples âmes, Marguerite de Porette, was burned in 1310. Also burned were the writings of the Ranters, against whom, in England in the seventeenth century, the same accusations were made as against the Libre Esprit several centuries earlier. See Norman Cohn, The Pursuit of the Millennium: Revolutionary Millenarians and Mystical Anarchists of the Middle Ages, revised and expanded edition (London: Temple Smith, 1970), p. 150.

5. "Sage mir, was du vom Übersetzen hälst, und ich sage dir wer du bist." Immediately afterwards the matter is raised of the translation, which is itself "deinon," of the deinon: "furchtbar," "gewaltig," "ungewöhnlich," and, in less "correct" but "more true" fashion, says Heidegger, "unheimlich." ("Die Bedeutung des deinon," in Gesamtausgabe, Bd. 53, pp. 74ff.) I invoke this passage because the enigma of the deinon leaves its mark on all the texts we shall have to approach.

CHAPTER II

1. "Le puits et la pyramide: Introduction à la sémiologie de Hegel," in *Marges—de la philosophie* (Paris: Minuit, 1972), pp. 79–127 [trans. Alan Bass, *Margins of Philosophy* (University of Chicago Press, 1982), pp. 69–108]. *Glas* (Paris: Galilée 1974) [trans. John P. Leavey, Jr., and Richard Rand (University of Nebraska Press, 1986)] treats the word and concept of *Geist* in Hegel as its most explicit theme.

2. "Heidegger," *Cahiers de l'Herne* 45 (1983), pp. 419–30, reprinted in *Psyché*, pp. 395–414 [trans. in *Research in Phenomenology* 13 (1983), 65–83].

3. They were Thomas Keenan, Thomas Levine, Thomas Pepper, and Andrzej Warminski. I want to express here my gratitude to them; this book is dedicated to them, as well as to Alexander Garcia Düttmann, in memory of "Schelling."

4. "*Denn das Fragen ist die Frömmigkeit des Denkens*": "For questioning is the piety of thought." This is the last sentence of "Die Frage nach der Technik" (1953) in *Vorträge und Aufsätze* (Pfullingen: Neske, 1954), pp. 13–44 [trans. William Lovitt, in *Martin Heidegger: Basic Writings*, ed. David Farrell Krell (London: Routledge, 1978), pp. 287–317]. A little earlier, Heidegger had just determined, in a way, what he understood by the word "pious" (*fromm*). At this point he writes of art when it had no other name than *tekhnè*: "It was a single, manifold revealing (*einziges, vielfältiges Entbergen*). It was pious (*fromm*), *promos* [what comes in the first rank, at the head], i.e. yielding to the holding sway and the safekeeping of truth (*fügsam dem Walten und Verwahren der Wahrheit*)" (p. 38 [316]).

5. "What is unthought in a thinker's thought is not a lack inherent in his thought. What is *un*-thought is there in each case only as the un-*thought*." *What Is Called Thinking?*, trans. Fred D. Wieck and J. Glenn Gray (New York: Harper and Row, 1968), p. 76. See too on this point "Désistance," in *Psyché*, pp. 615ff.

6. No doubt earlier than *Glas*, one of whose themes it is. See pp. 35 [27], 163 [144], and passim. See too *La Carte postale* (Paris: Aubier-Flammarion, 1981), p. 502, n. 20 [trans. Alan Bass, *The Post Card* (University of Chicago Press, 1987), p. 474, n. 51].

7. Given as a seminar in Paris and as a lecture at a conference at

Loyola University (Chicago), subsequently published in English as "*Geschlecht* II: Heidegger's Hand," in *Deconstruction and Philosophy*, ed. John Sallis (Chicago: University of Chicago Press, 1986). The French version of this lecture can be found in *Psyché*, pp. 415–51.

8. *Parmenides*, Gesamtausgabe, Bd. 54, pp. 118ff.

9. *Die Grundbegriffe der Metaphysik*, Gesamtausgabe, Bd. 29/30, §§44ff.

10. "What Is Called Thinking?" p. 76.

CHAPTER III

1. "Introduction" to *The Philosophy of Spirit*, in the Encyclopedia, §378. In the same introduction, Hegel defines the essence of spirit as *liberty* and as the capacity, in its formal determination, to support *infinite suffering*. I think I must quote this paragraph to anticipate what will be said later about spirit, liberty, and evil for Heidegger: "This is why the essence of spirit is formally *liberty*, the absolute negativity of the concept as self-identity. According to this formal determination, it can abstract all that is exterior and its own exteriority, its own presence: it can support the negation of its individual immediacy, infinite *suffering:* that is, conserve itself affirmative in this negation and be identical for itself. This possibility is in itself the abstract universality of spirit, universality which-is-for-itself" (§ 382).

CHAPTER V

1. *The Self-Assertion of the German University* [trans. Karsten Harries, *Review of Metaphysics*, 38, no. 3 (1985), 470–80(473). German/French bilingual edition (Toulouse: T.E.R., 1982), p. 10. Hereafter first reference is to this edition.

2. "Who Is Nietzsche's Zarathustra?" *Vorträge und Aufsätze* (Pfullingen: Neske, 1954 [2 ed., 1959], pp. 101–26, (p. 121) [trans. in *Nietzsche*, 4 vols (London: Routledge and Kegan Paul, 1981–87), vol. 2, pp. 211–33 (p. 288)]. Of course, this is not a "reproach," nor even a refutation. Heidegger always denies doing this. He never criticizes or refutes. This is, according to him, the "game of the

smallminded" (*Kleingeisterei*), as he explains precisely after the passage I have just quoted and the question he asks in it (p. 121 [229]). He had first of all applauded Nietzsche for thinking revenge "metaphysically"—the dimension of revenge not being primarily "moral" or "psychological" (p. 112 [221]). Then he sketches the movement leading to the limit of Nietzsche's thought as the accomplishment of metaphysics, in the place where something appears in Nietzsche's thought which it can no longer think. And it is precisely the spirit of revenge (*Geist der Rache*), which would perhaps not be overcome (merely "spiritualized to the highest degree") by this discourse on the imprint (*Aufprägen*), that Nietzsche talks about: "*Dem Werden den Charakter des Seins* aufzuprägen—*das ist der* höchste Wille zur Macht" (p. 120 [228]).

3. This liberty of spirit always runs the risk rigorously determined by the Hegel text quoted above (n. 1, chap. 3): that of a merely formal liberty and of an abstract universality.

4. "*Jede wesentliche Gestalt des Geistes steht in der Zweideutigkeit*" (p. 7; [trans. R. Manheim, *Introduction to Metaphysics* (New Haven: Yale University Press, 1959), p. 9].

5. The indictment of America, its "pseudo-philosophy" and its "patented psychology," etc., continues for a long time, no doubt reaching its apogee in 1941. See *Grundbegriffe* (Gesamtausgabe, Bd. 51), pp. 84 and 92.

CHAPTER VI

1. Gesamtausgabe, Bd. 29/30, p. 276.

2. "Le chant de la terre" (*The Song of the Earth*), *Cahiers de l'Herne* (1987), p. 70.

3. If animals cannot properly question beyond their vital interests, can *Dasein, properly and in all rigor?* Can it not be demonstrated that the question does no more than *defer*, indeed by the most overdetermined means (through difference *and différance* of difference) the quest and the inquiry, thus only *deflecting* living interest, with alteration and the most discontinuous mutation thus also remaining just a detour? Only being-for-death *as such* can seem to suspend and liberate the question in its rootedness in life. And this is doubtless what Heidegger would say. Later, he was to

stress that animals cannot have experience (*erfahren*) of "death as death." Which is why they cannot speak (*Unterwegs zur Sprache* [Pfullingen: Neske, 1959], p. 215) [trans. Peter D. Hertz, *On the Way to Language* (New York: Harper and Row, 1971), p. 107]. But does *Dasein* have experience of death *as such*, even by anticipation? What could that mean? What is being-for-death? What is death for a *Dasein* that is never defined *essentially* as a living thing? This is not a matter of opposing death to life, but of wondering what semantic content can be given to death in a discourse for which the relation to death, the experience of death, remains unrelated to the life of the living thing. (The problem of life was broached by Didier Franck at this same conference. See too "Geschlecht," in *Psyché*, p. 411.)

CHAPTER VII

1. "Philosophy and the Crisis of European Humanity," in *The Crisis of European Sciences and Phenomenology*, Husserliana, Bd. VI, pp. 318ff. (p. 352) [trans. David Carr (Evanston: Northwestern University Press, 1970), pp. 269–99 (p. 273)]. This figure of Europe is, precisely, "spiritual," in that it is no longer assigned a geographical or territorial outline. It is what gives its name to the "unity of a spiritual life, action, and creation." Can this "spiritual" determination of European humanity be reconciled with the exclusion of "Eskimoes, Indians, travelling zoos or gypsies permanently wandering all over Europe"? Right after asking the question "How is the spiritual figure of Europe to be characterized?" Husserl adds: "*Im geistigen Sinn gehören offenbar die englischen Dominions, die Vereinigten Staaten usw. zu Europa, nicht aber die Eskimos oder Indianer der Jahrmarktsmenagerien oder die Zigeuner, die dauernd in Europa herumvagabundieren.*" The retention of the English colonies in "spiritual" Europe would be proof of a ludicrous enough kind—by the comic load weighing down this sinister passage—of a philosophical non-sequitur whose gravity can be measured in two dimensions: (1) It is apparently necessary, therefore, in order to save the English dominions, the power and culture they represent, to make a distinction between, for example, good and bad Indians. This is not very "logical," either in "spiritualist"

logic or in "racist" logic. (2) This text was delivered in 1935 in Vienna!

Why is it necessary to recall this passage and quote it today? For several reasons. (1) On the basis of an example taken from a discourse which in general is not suspected of the worst, it is useful to recall that the reference to *spirit*, to the *freedom* of spirit, and to spirit as *European* spirit could and still can ally itself with the politics one would want to oppose to it. And this reference to spirit, and to Europe, is no more an external or accidental ornament for Husserl's thought than it is for Heidegger's. It plays a major, organizing role in the transcendental teleology of reason as Europocentric humanism. The question of the animal is never very far away: "just as man, *and even the Papuan* [my emphasis—J.D.] represents a new stage in animality in contrast to the animals, so philosophical reason represents a new stage in humanity and in its reason" (*Krisis* . . . , quoted in my Introduction to the *Origin of Geometry* [Paris: PUF, 1962]; trans. John P. Leavey, Jr. [Brighton: Harvester, 1978], p. 162 [p. 146], to which I take leave to refer the reader here). The "new stage" is clearly that of European humanity. It is (ought to be) traversed by the *telos* of transcendental phenomenology as, for Heidegger, it ought to be by the responsibility of the originary questioning on Being, beyond even transcendental subjectivity and the *animal rationale*. (2) Husserl and Heidegger are often, quite rightly, placed in opposition, not only in their thought but in their political history. Although he contests the facts or the stories, Heidegger is often accused of having participated in the persecutions suffered by Husserl. And the fact remains, beyond any possible contestation, that he erased (he didn't cross out this time, he erased) the dedication of *Sein und Zeit* to Husserl so that the book could be republished, in a gesture which reconstitutes the erasure as an unerasable, mediocre, and hideous crossing-out. This isn't the place to deal with these problems and facts in their full scope. But it is right that there should *not be too many* lacunae or injustices in this interminable trial, constantly being extended with new evidence. Under the rubric of spirit and of Europe—since this is our only subject here—we must not forget what certain "victims" wrote and thought. And still in the name of spirit. Would Heidegger have subscribed to what Husserl said of the gypsies?

Would he have thrown the "non-Aryans" out of Europe, as did he who knew he was himself "non-Aryan," i.e. Husserl? And if the reply is "no," to all appearances "no," is it certain that this is for reasons other than those which distanced him from transcendental idealism? Is what he did or wrote worse? Where is the worse? That is perhaps the question *of spirit*.

2. *Variété* (Paris: Gallimard, 1924), p. 32. The comparative analysis of these three discourses—Valéry's, Husserl's and Heidegger's—on the crisis or destitution of spirit as spirit of Europe, would bring out an odd configuration, and paradigmatic features which are exchanged in a regulated way. Valéry sometimes seems closer to Husserl, sometimes closer to Heidegger, sometimes far from both. He speaks of "the lost illusion of a European culture" (p. 16). He begins by evoking ash and ghosts [*revenants*]. "We knew quite well that all the apparent earth was made of ashes, that ash signifies something. We perceived through the breadth of history the ghosts of immense ships loaded with wealth and spirit" (pp. 11–12). Further on is the famous passage about "the immense terrace of Elsinore, which stretches from Basle to Cologne, which touches the sands of Nieuport, the marshes of the Somme, the chalk of Champagne, the granite of Alsace," all those places from which "the European Hamlet watches million of specters" (p. 19:this was only in 1919). Then Valéry distinguishes the European Hamlet from his double, "an intellectual Hamlet," who "meditates on the life and death of truths. His ghosts are all the objects of our disputes" and he "does not really know what to do with all these skulls" (Leonardo, Leibniz, Kant, Hegel, Marx): "Farewell, ghosts! The world no longer needs you. Nor me. The world, which baptizes with the name of progress its tendency toward a fatal precision, seeks to unite to the favors of life the advantages of death. A certain confusion reigns still, but a little more time and everything will become clear; we shall in the end see the appearance of the miracle of an animal society, a perfect and definitive ant-hill" (pp. 20–22). Later, in 1932, in "La Politique de l'esprit, notre souverain bien" ["The Politics of Spirit—our Sovereign Good"] (*Variété III* [Paris: Gallimard, 1936], pp. 193–228), Valéry proposes what is, all in all, a rather classical, or even neo-Hegelian, negative-dialectic definition of spirit as that which in the end "always says no," and first of all no to itself. Valéry says of this definition that it is not "meta-

physical," by which he means, very metaphysically, a physical, economic, energetic power of transformation and opposition: "But I must now complete this picture of disorder and this composition of chaos, by showing you that which sees it and feeds it, can neither stand it nor deny it, and, in its essence, never stops dividing against itself. I mean *spirit*. By this name "spirit," I do not at all mean a metaphysical entity [look at Valéry's invisible quotation marks]; I here mean very simply a *power of transformation* which we can isolate [. . .] by considering [. . .] certain modifications [. . .] which we can attribute only to an action very different from that of the energies of nature; for it consists on the contrary in opposing to each other those energies which are given to us, or else in linking them together. This opposition or coercion is such that there results from it either a gain of time, or a saving of our own forces, or an increase in power, precision, freedom, or duration for our lives" (pp. 216–17). The negative economy of spirit which is none other than the origin of its freedom, opposes spirit to life and makes consciousness into a "spirit of spirit." But this spirit always remains *man's*. Man "thus acts *against nature*, and his action is one of those opposing *spirit* to *life* [. . .]. He has acquired to different degrees *self-consciousness*, that consciousness which means that, in occasionally moving away from *all that is*, he can even move away from his own personality; the *self* can sometimes consider its own person as an almost foreign object. Man can observe himself (or thinks he can); he can criticize himself, constrain himself; that's an original creation, an attempt to create what I shall venture to call *the spirit of spirit*" (pp. 220–21). It is true that this opposition of spirit and life is sometimes apprehended as a simple phenomenon, or even an appearance: "Thus spirit seems to abhor and flee the very processes of deep organic life [. . .]. Spirit, in this way, indeed opposes itself to the running of the life-machine [. . .] it develops the fundamental law [. . .] of sensibility" (pp. 222–23).

Under the brilliant singularity of Valéry's aphorism or *trait d'esprit*, one recognizes those profound invariables, those repetitions which their author opposes, precisely, as nature to spirit. The philosophemes come under the same program and the same combinatory as those of Hegel, Husserl, and Heidegger. There is simply dissociation or permutation of the features concerned. For example: (1) If it is opposed to nature and life, spirit is history and "in general, *happy peoples have no spirit.* They don't much need it" (p. 237). (2) Europe is not defined by geography or empirical history: "You will excuse my giving to these words 'Europe' and 'European' a signification slightly more than geographical, slightly more than historical, but as it were, *functional*" (*Variété,* p. 41). Only this last word would have provoked the protests of the other participants in this great and fabulous European colloquium—and especially of the Germans: this functionalism is both too naturalistic and too technicist, too "objectivist," "mechanistic," "Cartesian," etc. (3) Crisis as destitution of spirit: "What then is this spirit? In what way can it be touched, struck, diminished, humiliated by the current state of the world? Whence this great pity of the things of spirit, this distress, this anguish of the men of spirit?" (*Variété,* p. 34; see too "La Liberté de l'esprit" ["The Freedom of Spirit"] [1939], in *Oeuvres,* ed. Jean Hytier, 2 vols. [Paris: Gallimard, 1960], II, pp. 1077–99). And this is indeed what they are all wondering, in this imaginary symposium, in this invisible university where, for more than twenty years, the greatest European minds [*esprits*] met. They echo each other, discuss or translate the same admiring anguish: "*So,* what is happening to us? *So,* what is happening to Europe? *So,* what is happening to Spirit? Where is it coming to us from? Is it still from *spirit?*"

And, to conclude, ash: "Knowledge having devoured everything, no longer knowing what to do, consider this little pile of ashes and this wisp of smoke it made of the Cosmos and a cigarette" (*Cahiers* [26], p. 26).

3. Beda Allemann, for example, writes: "*Spirit* is one of those words which Heidegger only uses in quotation marks after *Being and Time.* It is one of the fundamental expressions of absolute Metaphysics" (*Hölderlin und Heidegger,* 2d ed. [Zurich: Atlantis, 1954], p. 167). It is the opposite which is true, and massively so, as we are constantly confirming. After *Sein und Zeit,* precisely, Heidegger no longer writes *spirit* in quotation marks. There is even, as we shall shortly see, an instance of him effacing the quotation marks retroactively in an earlier publication, the *Rectorship Address.*

4. I am quoting from Gérard Granel's translation (p. 13), since I did so above for the same passage. It differs considerably from that

of Gilbert Kahn in the *Introduction*. But the difference obviously has nothing to do with the play of quotation marks.

5. "Martin Heidegger interrogé par *Der Spiegel*. Réponses et questions sur l'histoire et la politique" ["Martin Heidegger Interviewed by *Der Spiegel*: Responses and Questions on History and Politics," trans. William J. Richardson, S.J. as "'Only a God Can Save us': The *Spiegel* Interview," in T. Sheehan, ed, *Heidegger, the Man and the Thinker* (Chicago: Precedent Publishing, 1981), pp. 45–67 (p. 62)], trans. Jean Launay (Mercure de France, 1977), pp. 66–67.

6. Fichte, *Reden an die deutsche Nation* (Hamburg: Felix Reiner Verlag. 1978). p. 122.

7. *Schellings Abhandlung Über des Wesen der menschlichen Freiheit (1809)* (Tübingen: Niemeyer, 1971), p. 154 [trans. Joan Stambaugh, *Schelling's Treatise on the Essence of Human Freedom* (Athens, Ohio: Ohio University Press, 1985), p. 128].

8. As we were suggesting above, all this seems "a little comical," despite the seriousness of the issues. To remain sensitive to this humor, still to be able to laugh at some move or other, could become an obligation (political or ethical, if one so wishes), and a chance, despite the suspicions explicitly loaded onto the *Witz*, or *wit*, or the French *esprit* [joke], the chance *de l'esprit*, by so many German philosophers. In this concert of European languages, we can already hear Greek, German, Latin, French. But let us at this point leave what perhaps remains too close to the European *center*, constrained, compressed in the "vice," oppressed and even repressed in the "middle." For the purposes of being able to take a breather, is not *eccentricity* de rigueur? So I will recall in the original language Matthew Arnold's English wit. Readers of *Friendship's Garland* will remember "the great doctrine of *Geist*," and how in Letter I, "I introduce Arminius and 'Geist' to the British public." A few fragments to encourage the reading or rereading of someone who, even in the nineteenth century, was not completely deaf to a certain untranslatability of *Geist*. At any rate, he realized he should leave *Geist* untouched in its language: "'Liberalism and despotism!' cried the Prussian; 'let us go beyond these forms and words. What unites and separates people now is *Geist*. . . . There you will find that in Berlin we oppose 'Geist,'—*intelligence*, as you or the French might say,—to 'Ungeist.' The victory of 'Geist' over

'Ungeist' we think the great matter in the world. . . . We North-Germans have worked for 'Geist' in our way . . . in your middle class 'Ungeist' is rampant; and as for your aristocracy, you know 'Geist' is forbidden by nature to flourish in an aristocracy. . . . What has won this Austrian battle for Prussia is 'Geist'. . . I will give you this piece of advice, with which I take my leave: '*Get Geist*'."
"Thank God, this d——d professor (to speak as Lord Palmerston) is now gone back to his own *Intelligenz-Staat*. I half hope there may next come a smashing defeat of the Prussians before Vienna, and make my ghostly friend laugh on the wrong side of the mouth." Closely linked to *Culture and Anarchy*, these twelve fictional letters were collected into a book in 1871. Arnold took great pleasure in playing the role of editor and in writing footnotes: "I think it is more self-important and *bête* if I put Ed. after every note. It is rather fun making the notes." This was a letter to his publisher: *bête* is italicized, because it is in French in the text, as *esprit* is in Kant's *Anthropology* (see above). It is what I would like to stress in my turn. And that this fable of *Geist* go by the lips of a spirit of this "ghostly friend" one would like to get to laugh, "half hope," "on the wrong side of his mouth."

By the way [in English in the text], *Get Geist* is barely translatable into French, and not only because of *Geist*, but because of *Get. Profoundly* untranslatable is the hidden profundity of the word *Get* which means *have, become* and *be,* all three. *Get Geist*: (1) have, obtain, gain, or apprehend (some) *Geist.* (2) Be or become, learn how to become, *yourself, Geist.* And *Geist* then functions as an attribute (become "spirit" as one would say "get mad," "get drunk," "get married," "get sick," "get well" or "get better" and as a noun ("get religion," convert yourself)—in short, *become or have, yourself, spirit itself.* Do we not see the resistance of this untranslatability—the sameness in the relation to itself, in itself, of a *Geist* which is what it has, becomes what it has or ought to have been—thus transferred, by a *trait d'esprit* and underhandedly [*sous la manche:* also "under the [English] Channel"—trans.], on the other side [*à gauche:* literally, "to (or on) the left"], towards the *first word,* i.e. the *verb* in the Babelian sentence: *Get Geist!* The wit [*esprit*] depends on the performative and entirely initial force of these two words: injunction, demand, prayer, desire, advice, order, prescription. No report precedes the mark of spirit, no history can have preceded this remarkable *trait d'esprit.* Culture and anarchy. In the beginning—no beginning [*pas de commencement:* also "a beginning step"]. Spirit apostrophizes itself in *this verb,* it addresses it to itself and says (*to*) *itself,* says it to itself, let it say it to itself and let it be well understood: in the beginning, there will have been, ghost of the future perfect, *Get Geist: de l'esprit.*

CHAPTER VIII

1. *Nietzsche,* 2 vols. (Pfullingen: Neske, 1961), vol. 2, p. 200 [vol. 4, p. 148].

2. Gesamtausgabe, Bd. 53, pp. 156ff.

3. "The work of spirit, according to the doctrine of modern Idealism, is the act of positing (*das Setzen*). Because spirit is conceived of as subject and thus is represented (*vorgestellt*) within the subject-object schema, the act of positing (Thesis) must be the synthesis between the subject and its objects" (*Unterwegs zur Sprache,* p. 248 [118]).

4. Also, perhaps, in the constant reading of Meister Eckhart, who says for example: "Now Augustine says that, in the upper part of the soul, which is called *mens* or *gemüte,* God created, at the same time as the being of the soul, a power (*craft*) which the masters call receptacle (*sloz*) or case (*schrin*) of spiritual forms or formal images ["ideas"]." *Renovamini . . . spiritu mentis vestrae,* trans. Jeanne Ancelet-Hustache, in *Sermons* (Paris: Seuil, 1979), vol. III, p. 151. See too *Psyché,* pp. 583ff.

5. Allemann, *Hölderlin und Heidegger,* p. 167.

6. The truth of quotation marks: this equivocation is concentrated in the interpretation of the quotation marks in which Nietzsche encloses the word "truth" (see *Nietzsche,* vol. I, pp. 511ff. [vol. 3, pp. 34ff].

CHAPTER IX

1. "Die Sprache im Gedicht, Eine Erörterung von Georg Trakls Gedicht" (1953), in *Unterwegs zur Sprache,* pp. 39ff. [159–98].

2. P. 70 [188]. The necessary path would here lead from speech

to saying (*sagen*), from saying to poetic saying (*Dichten*), from *Dichten* to song (*Singen, Gesang*), to the accord of consonance (*Einklang*), from this to the *hymn* and thus to *praise*. I am not here pointing to an order of logical consequences, nor to the necessity to *regress* from one meaning to another. It is merely a question of pointing to a problematic in which I cannot get involved here (I try to do so elsewhere: see "Comment ne pas parler," in *Psyché*, pp. 570ff.) and in which these meanings appear indissociable for Heidegger. The hymn exceeds the ontological, theoretical or constative utterance. It calls to praise, it sings praise beyond what is, and perhaps even—we'll come back to this later—beyond that form of "piety" of thought that Heidegger one day called the question, questioning (*Fragen*). In this text, Heidegger entrusts his whole interpretation, at decisive moments, to the place of and listening to a tone, a word which carries the *Grundton*, and this is the stressed (*betont*) word: "one," *Ein* in "Ein *Geschlecht*. . . ." (*Dieses betonte* "Ein *Geschlecht*" birgt den *Grundton*. . . .) p. 78. He ceaselessly appeals to listen to what the poem says insofar as it sings it in a *Gesang*. This word is sometimes translated as *hymn* but Heidegger also insists on the value of gathering. The *Gesang* is all at once (*in einem*), he says, "*Lied*, tragedy, and *epos*" (p. 65)). A few years later, Heidegger specifies further this link between the song (*Lied*) and the hymn (the act of honoring, praising, *laudare*, singing the praises). Praise is always sung. On *Das Lied*, by Stefan George: "Thinking—assembling—loving, such is the saying: peacefully incline oneself in the happiness of joyfulness, venerate in jubilation (*ein jubelndes Verehren*), celebrate (*ein Preisen*), sing the praise (*ein Loben*): *laudare*. *Laudes* is the Latin word for songs (*Laudes lautet der lateinische Name für die Lieder*). Saying songs means singing (*Leider sagen heisst: singen*). Plainsong (*der Gesang*) is the gathering of song (*die Versammlung des Sagens in das Lied*). ("Das Wort," in *Unterwegs* . . . , p. 229 [148]. See too "Der Weg zur Sprache" [1959], this time on Hölderlin, on *Gespräch* and *Gesang*, in *Unterwegs* . . . , p. 226 [135].)

3. Pp. 59, 77 [175, 194]. See too "Hölderlins Erde und Himmel," in *Erläuterung zu Hölderlins Dichtung*, 5th ed. (Frankfurt: Klostermann, 1981), pp. 152–81 (p. 153). For everything we are discussing here, see too pp. 43–46, 50, 56–60, 64–68, 84–94, 120–23, 175, and passim.

4. Paul de Man, *Allegories of Reading* (New Haven: Yale University Press, 1979), Chapter 11, "Promises (Social Contract)," p. 277. I have addressed these problems and cited some of Heidegger's references to the promise in *Mémoires—for Paul de Man* (New York: Columbia University Press, 1986), Chapter 3, "Acts: The Meaning of a Given Word," pp. 91–153 (pp. 95ff).

5. Before any question, then. It is precisely here that the "question of the question" which has been dogging us since the beginning of this journey, vacillates. It vacillates at this moment when it is no longer a question. Not that it withdraws from the infinite legitimacy of questioning, but it tips over into the memory of a language, of an experience of language "older" than it, always anterior and presupposed, old enough never to have been present in an "experience" or a "speech act"—in the usual sense of these words. This moment—which is not a moment—is *marked* in Heidegger's text. When he speaks of the promise and the *"es gibt,"* of course, and at least implicitly, but in literal and extremely explicit fashion in "Das Wesen der Sprache," in *Unterwegs . . . ,* especially pp. 174ff. [71ff.]. Everything begins from the question mark (*Fragezeichen*) when one interrogates the essence of language. What is the essence of language? The essence (*das Wesen*)? of language (*der Sprache*)? Schematically: at the moment at which we pose the ultimate question, i.e. when we interrogate (*Anfragen*) the possibility of any question, i.e. language, we must be *already* in the element of language. Language must already be speaking for us—it must, so to speak, be already spoken and addressed to us (*muss uns doch die Sprache selber schon zugesprochen sein*). *Anfrage* and *Nachfrage* presuppose this advance, this fore-coming [*prévenante*] address (*Zuspruch*) of language. Language is *already* there, in advance (*im voraus*) at the moment at which any question can arise about it. In this it exceeds the question. This advance is, before any contract, a sort of promise of originary alliance to which we must have in some sense already acquiesced, already said *yes*, given a pledge [*gage*], whatever may be the negativity or problematicity of the discourse which may follow. This promise, this reply which is produced a priori in the form of acquiescence, this commitment of language towards language, this giving of language by language and to language is what Heidegger at this point regularly names *Zusage*. And it is in the name of this *Zusage* that he again puts in

question, if one can still call it this, the ultimate authority, the supposed last instance of the questioning attitude. I will not translate the word *Zusage* because it brings together meanings which in general we keep separate: promise, agreement or consent, originary abandonment to what is given in the promise itself. "What is our experience (*was erfahren wir*) when we sufficiently meditate (*bedenken*) on this? That questioning (*Fragen*) is not the gesture proper to thinking (*die eigentliche Gebärde des Denkens*) [the word *Gebärde*, gesture and gestation, is itself a theme of meditation elsewhere, p. 22—"Language," trans. Albert Hofstadter in *Poetry, Language, Thought* (New York: Harper and Row, 1971), pp. 189–210 (p. 200)], but—listening to the *Zusage* of what must come to the question" (p. 175 [71]).

The question is thus not the last word in language. First, because it is not the first word. At any rate, before the word, there is this sometimes wordless word which we name the "yes." A sort of pre-originary pledge [*gage*] which precedes any other engagement in language or action. But the fact that it precedes language does not mean that it is foreign to it. The *gage* engages in language—and so always in *a* language. The question itself is thus pledged—which does not mean linked or constrained, reduced to silence, on the contrary—by the pledge of *Zusage*. It answers in advance, and whatever it does, to this pledge and of this pledge. It is engaged by it in a responsibility it has not chosen and which assigns it even its liberty. The pledge will have been given before any other event. It is nonetheless, in its very coming before, an *event*, but an event of which the memory (*mémoire*) comes before any particular recollection (*souvenir*) and to which we are linked by a faith which defeats any narrative. No erasure is possible for such a pledge. No going back.

After recalling the fact that, in the history of our thought, questioning would be the trait (*Zug*) which gives thought its measure—because thought was first of all foundational, always in quest of the fundamental and the radical—Heidegger returns to one of his previous statements. Not, indeed, to put it in question, still less to contradict it, but to reinscribe it in a movement which exceeds it: "At the end of a lecture entitled *The Question Concerning Technology*, it was said some time ago: 'For questioning (*das Fragen*) is the piety (*Frömmigheit*) of thought'. Pious (*fromm*) is understood here in the old sense of 'docile' (*fügsam*), that is, docile to what thought has to think. It is a feature of the experiences which provoke thought that sometimes thought does not sufficiently take stock of the insights it has just gained, by failing to get the measure of them, to think them through. This is the case with the sentence quoted: 'questioning is the piety of thought'" (pp. 175–76 [72]).

On the basis of this, the whole lecture "Das Wesen der Sprache" will be ordered according to this thinking of *Zusage*. It is understandable that Heidegger denies proceeding to an artificial and formal, "empty" "reversal" (*Umkehrung*). But it has to be admitted that the thought of an affirmation anterior to any question and more proper to thought than any question must have an unlimited incidence—nonlocalizable, without possible circumscription—on the *quasi*-totality of Heidegger's previous path of thought. It is not an *Umkehrung*, but it is something other than a turning (*Kehre*). The turning still belongs to the question. Heidegger says this explicitly. This step transforms or deforms (as you like) the whole landscape to the extent that that landscape had been constituted *before* [devant] *the*—inflexible—*law* of the most radical questioning. Limiting myself to a few indications among many, let me recall that the point of departure of the analytic of *Dasein*—and therefore the project of *Sein und Zeit* itself—was assigned by the opening of *Dasein* to the question; and that the whole *Destruktion* of ontology took as its target, especially in post-Cartesian modernity, an inadequate questioning of the Being of the subject, etc. This retrospective upheaval can seem to dictate a new *order*. One would say, for example, that now everything has to be begun again, taking as the point of departure the en-gage [*l'en-gage*: cf. *langage*] of the *Zusage* so as to construct a quite different discourse, open a quite different path of thought, proceed to a new *Kehre* if not to an *Umkehrung*, and remove—a highly ambiguous gesture—the remnant of *Aufklärung* which still slumbered in the privilege of the question. In fact, without believing that we can henceforth not take account of this profound upheaval, we cannot take seriously the imperative of such a recommencement. For a number of reasons:

1. First of all, this would involve a complete lack of understanding of the irreversible necessity of a path which, from the vantage of the narrow and perilous passage to which it leads thinking, per-

mits, very late on, to see differently, at a given moment, its unique past (breaching, path of language and writing) which inscribes in it all the rest, including the passage in question, the passage beyond the question. Even if one can retrace one's steps, thanks precisely to this discovered passage, the return does not signify a new departure, from a new principle or some degree zero.

2. A new point of departure would not only be impossible, it would make no sense for a thinking which never submitted to the law of the system and even made the systematic in philosophy into one of its most explicit themes and questions.

3. The order to which Heidegger's path of thought entrusts itself was never an "order of reasons." What sustains such an order in Descartes, for example, calls forth the questions we have already discussed.

These are so many reasons for not re-commencing when it is already too late, always too late. And the structure of this gage can thus be translated: "it is already too late, always too late." Once these reasons have been understood, retrospection can, indeed *must*, instead of disqualifying or recommencing everything, lead to another strategy and another stratigraphy. Heidegger's journey crosses, constitutes, or leaves certain strata up until now scarcely visible, less massive, sometimes almost imperceptible—for Martin Heidegger as much as for anyone. In their rarity, precariousness, or very discretion, these strata appear prominent after the event, to the extent that they restructure a space. But they do this only by assigning so many new tasks to thought, and to reading. All the more so in that, in the example which concerns us here, it is precisely a question of the very origin of responsibility. This is much more, and other, than an example. On the basis of which one can search , in the whole of Heidegger's work, *before* there is any question of the gage of the *Zusage* in language, *before* any question of the en-gage, *before* the privilege of the question is placed in question, *before* 1958—if one wants a date—for markers and signs allowing one to situate in advance and in its necessity the passage thus discovered. These signs and markers exist, and we are better prepared now to recognize them, interpret them, reinscribe them. And this is useful not only for *reading* Heidegger and serving some hermeneutical or philological piety. Beyond an always necessary exegesis, this re-reading sketches out another topology for new tasks, for what remains to be situated of the relationships between Heidegger's thought and other places of thought—or of the engage—places which one pictures as regions but which are not (ethics or politics, but also, again, philosophy, science, all the sciences and, immediately, those unstable and unsituatable discourses—linguistics, poetics, pragmatics, psychoanalysis, etc.)

What, retrospectively, could these signs and markers be? In a note such as this I can only point to a few of them among others, in the driest of fashions.

A. Everything in *Sein und Zeit* (§§58,59,60) which concerns the sense of the "appeal" (*Rufsinn*) and imputability (rather than responsibility or culpability), the "*Schuldigsein*" before any "moral consciousness."

B. Everything in *Sein und Zeit* and the *Introduction to Metaphysics* which concerns *Entschlossenheit* and the possibility of assuming (*Übernehmen*) the mission (*Sendung*) (*Introduction to Metaphysics*, p. 38 [50]) and therefore the originary questioning it assigns. The opening to the assignment of the question, responsibility, resolution with respect to the question are necessarily presupposed by questioning itself. They are not confused with it. The question is not suspended but sustained *by* this other piety, *held* and dependent *on* it [*La question n'est pas suspendue mais soutenue par cette autre piété, tenue et suspendue à elle*].

C. Everything which concerns *Verlässlichkeit*, a certain originary "trustworthiness," in *The Origin of the Work of Art* (permit me to refer here to *La Vérité en peinture* (Paris: Flammarion, 1979), pp. 398ff. [trans. Geoff Bennington and Ian McLeod, *The Truth in Painting* (University of Chicago Press, 1987), pp. 349ff.].

D. Everything which concerns the "yes" and the "no," the saying (*Sagen*) of which is not primarily a logical or propositional statement (*Aussagen*)—in the passage from the course on *Schelling* which, moreover, deals symmetrically with affirmation and negation (p. 143 [p. 119]).

E. Everything which concerns the promise (*Versprechen* or *Verheissen*), for example in *Was Heisst Denken?* (see above, n. 4).

But since my purpose bound me to privilege the modalities of avoiding (*vermeiden*)—and notably the silent dramaturgy of pragmatic signs (such as quotation marks or crossings-through), I move on to this third example of crossing through: that of a question mark. Heidegger had first suggested that the question mark after *Das Wesen?* or *der Sprache?* attenuated what might be pretentious or familiar in the title of a discourse on the essence of language. Now after having recalled that this con-fident listening to the *Zusage* was the very gesture of thought, its most proper scope or behavior (*Gebärde*), he concludes the necessity—a certain necessity not to be confused with dogmatic certainty—of crossing through again the question marks (*die Fragezeichen wieder streichen*) (p. 180 [76]).

[Pause for a moment: to dream of what the Heideggerian corpus would look like the day when, with all the application and consistency required, the operations prescribed by him at one moment or another would indeed have been carried out: "avoid" the word "spirit," at the very least place it in quotation marks, then cross through all the names referring to the world whenever one is speaking of something which, like the animal, has no *Dasein*, and therefore no or only a little world, then place the word "Being" everywhere under a cross, and finally cross through without a cross all the question marks when it's a question of language, i.e., indirectly, of everything, etc. One can imagine the surface of a text given over to the gnawing, ruminant, and silent voracity of such an animal-machine and its implacable "logic." This would not only be simply "without spirit," but a figure of evil. The perverse reading of Heidegger. End of pause.]

To the extent that, in this singular situation which relates it to a pledge of this kind, thought is a "listening" (*Hören*) and a letting-oneself-say (*Sichsagenlassen*), and not a questioning (*kein Fragen*), then, says Heidegger, "we must still cross through the question marks." Which, he adds, does not mean a return to the habitual form of the title. That is no longer possible. The "letting itself be said" which urges the crossing through of the question mark is not a passive docility, much less an uncritical compliance. But no more is it a negative activity busy submitting everything to a denial that crosses through [*une dénégation raturante*]. It subscribes. Before us, before everything, below or above everything, it inscribes the question, negation or denial, it en-gages them without limits in the correspondence with *langue* or *parole* (*Sprache*). *Parole* must *first* pray, address itself to us: put in us its trust, its confidence, depend on us, and even have *already* done it (*muss sich die Sprache zuvor uns zusagen oder gar schon zugesagt haben*). The *already* is essential here, saying something of the essence of this *parole* and of what en-gages in it. At the moment when, in the present, it entrusts or addresses itself to us, it has *already* done so, and this past never returns, never again becomes present, it always goes back to an older event which will have already engaged us in this subscribing to the en-gage. Towards this fore-coming address (*Zuspruch*). On two occasions, Heidegger writes this, which seems to defeat translation: *Die Sprache west als dieser Zuspruch* (pp. 180–81 [76]). At an interval of a few lines, the French translator offers two different formulations: (1) "Speech deploys itself as this addressed speech (*La parole se déploie en tant que cette parole adressée)*"; (2) "Speech deploys itself as this address (*La parole se déploie en tant que cette adresse*)." [The English translation also has two versions: 1. "Language persists as this avowal"; 2. "Language is active as this promise" (p. 76)—trans.] The two translations are correct, even if they are condemned to incompleteness and to trying in vain to be complete. Address here is at once the direction, the relation, practically the apostrophe of the relation to (*zu*), *and* the content of what is addressed with *concern* [*prévenance*] (one of the common meanings of *Zuspruch*: assistance, consolation, exhortation), in the always anterior concern of this appeal addressed to us. Not only in *parole* (*Sprache*), but in *langue* (*Sprache*), the en-gage engaging in a *langue* as much as in *parole*. *Parole* is engaged in *langue*. And what is *deployed* here (*west*) is the essence (*Wesen*) of *Sprache*. All language on *Wesen* must be redeployed otherwise on the basis of what is written in this way: "*Das Wesen der Sprache: Die Sprache des Wesens*" (p. 181 [76]). The colon erases a copula and does the job of crossing through. Crossing through of Being, of *Sein* and *ist*, not of *Wesen*. In place of this erasure or of this colon, the copula "is" would reintroduce confusion in this place and would relaunch the question just where it lets itself be exceeded.

Thought about *Ereignis* takes its bearings from this acquiescence which responds—en-gages—to the address. And the proper of man arrives only in this response or this responsibility. At least it does this when, and only when, man acquiesces, consents, gives himself to the address addressed to him, that is to *his* address, the one which only properly becomes his own in this response. After naming *Ereignis* in this context, Heidegger recalls that the *Zusage* does not wander around in the void. "It has already touched." (*Sie hat schon getroffen*). Who else but man? (*Denn der Mensch ist nur Mensch, insofern er dem Zuspruch der Sprache zugesagt, für die Sprache, sie zu sprechen, gebraucht ist*) (p. 196 [90]). At the Essex conference I referred to above, Françoise Dastur reminded me of this passage of *Unterwegs zur Sprache* which indeed passes question. I dedicate this note to her as a pledge of gratitude.

6. On this point, I permit myself to refer to *La mythologie blanche* in *Marges—de la philosophie* (Paris: Minuit, 1972), pp. 249–324 [207–71], and "Le retrait de la métaphore," in *Psyché: Inventions de l'autre* (Paris: Galilée, 1987), 63–93 [trans. *Enclitic*, 2:2 (1978), pp. 5–34].

CHAPTER X

1. *Glas*, especially pp. 14, 20, 22, 31, 70, 106, 262–63 [8, 14, 15, 24, 59, 91, 235]. Given that we are trying to mark the continuity of a tradition in those places where the thematics of fire, hearth, guard, and nation cross, it is appropriate to quote Hegel once again: "We shall see in the *history of philosophy* that in the *other countries of Europe*, where the sciences and the formation of intelligence have been cultivated with zeal and consideration, philosophy has, its name apart, *disappeared and perished in its very memory and idea, but is has been preserved as a particular property (Eigentümlichkeit)* of the German nation. We have received from nature the *superior mission (den höheren Beruf)* of being the guardians of the sacred fire *(die Bewahrer dieses heiligen Feuers)*, as the family of the Eumolpidae at Athens guarded the mysteries of Eleusis and the islanders of Samothrace had the charge of conserving and caring for a superior cult, as in the past the World-Spirit *(der Weltgeist)* reserved the Jewish nation for supreme consciousness so that it might rise up in the middle of that nation as a new spirit." *Lectures on the History of Philosophy* (Oxford: Clarendon Press, 1985), pp. 1–2. This speech had begun (*it too*) by evoking "all the forces of spirit," the "spirit of the world," and "pure spirituality." At this point, in the margin of this inaugural address to the university, Hegel alluded to the "pale ghost" (*schale Gespenst*) opposed to the seriousness and superior need of Prussian intelligence. On the in-

terpretation of Judaism by Hegel, see too *Glas*, pp. 43–105 and passim. And on what "links up with Heidegger's ghost," or what can happen, for example on the telephone, "with the ghost or *Geist* of Martin," see *La carte postale*, pp. 25–26 [21].

2. On the one hand, this could come back, up to a certain point and in traditional fashion, to the reservations formulated by Hegel as to *pneumatology* (see above, chap. 3, n. 1). But on the other hand, one could also contest the distinction between *pneuma* and the flame or gas of a fire whose meaning would be marked only in the word *Geist*. Things are certainly more entangled than this. One must first of all recall that, in the *De spiritu* (XV, 478a 15), Aristotle speaks of a "psychic fire." It is however true that *psyché* is not *pneuma*; and Aristotle associates *pneuma* rather with solar fire and heat, with the vapor and gas which are its natural effects. But beyond the immense problem opened up here by the determination of *physis*, it is difficult to dissociate absolutely *pneuma* from heat and fire, even if the source of that heat and fire remains as "natural" as the sun. I refer here to Hélène Ioannidi's rich analysis, "Qu'est-ce que le psychique?" in *Philosophia*, 15–6 (1985–86), pp. 286ff. For example the following, on the relationship between sperm and soul: "Animal warmth is not fire but *pneuma*, hot air, gas. The nature of *pneuma* is analogous to the astral element . . . 'fire engenders no animal, and it is clear that no being is formed in matter on fire, be it damp or dry. On the contrary, solar heat has the power to engender as does animal warmth, not only that which is manifested through sperm, but if some other natural residue is produced, it too possesses, no less than sperm, a vital principle.' Emitted by the male, the psychic principle is contained in the seminal body which the male emits. The psychic principle includes both what is inseparable from the body and that divine something, the intellect, which is independent of it." (On p. 294, the author adds in a note: "Under this term *pneuma*, according to a note of P. Louis's, Aristotle naturally understands vapor, gas, air, fluid.")

3. The references would be too numerous here. One of the most peculiar, in this context, would be to Franz Rosenzweig, and what he says of fire, spirit, blood, and promise in *The Star of Redemption* (London: Routledge and Kegan Paul, 1971), p. 298ff.

4. Here too the references would be too numerous and doubtless useless. Let us make clear however that Paul distinguishes between

the "psychic man" (*psychikos anthropos*)—also translated as *"animalis homo"* or "natural man"—and "spiritual man" (*pneumatikos*) (*spiritualis*). The former does not accept what comes from the spirit of God (*ta tou pneumatos tou theou*). Holy spirit which can also, as *pneuma*, be a *parole soufflée*. Matthew: "for it is not you who will speak; it is the Spirit of your father (*to pneuma tou patros*) which will speak in you" (10:20). *Pneuma* (*spiritus*) can be sacred (*hagion, sanctus*) or impure (*akatharton, immundus*) (see for example Matthew 12:43; Mark 1:26, 3:11, etc.).

To my knowledge, Heidegger alludes to the Holy Spirit (*pneuma hagion*) only once, in a different context. But fire is not far away. It is a question of *glossa, lingua, langue, language*, that family of words which also makes so difficult the translation of *Sprache*, all at once *parole, langage,* and *langue*. Heidegger notes that, from this point of view, *"Die Sprache ist die Zunge"* (speech—language—is tongue [*la parole—la langue—est la langue*]); and he quotes Luther's translation of the Vulgate: "' . . . And there appeared to them tongues (*Zungen*), dispersed (*zerteilt*) like fire (*wie von Feuer*) . . . and they began to preach with other tongues (*mit anderen Zungen*)'. Nonetheless this new capacity to discourse (*Reden*) is not understood as simple loquacity (*Zungenfertigkeit*, silver-tonguedness) but full of *pneuma hagion*, the sacred breath (*vom heiligen Hauch*)" (*Unterwegs zur Sprache*, p. 203 [96–7]).

5. After having recognized that it is "just as impossible in philosophy to return with a single leap to Greek philosophy as it is to abolish by decree the Christianity which entered Western history and consequently philosophy," after having specified that the beginning of philosophy was "grandiose" because it "had to overcome its most powerful antagonist, the mythical in general, and the Asiatic in particular," Heidegger adds: "It is certain that Schelling, from the treatise on freedom onwards, emphasizes more and more the positivity of Christianity; but having said that, one has still decided nothing with regard to the essence and signification of his metaphysical thinking, which thereby is still not understood, and even remains incomprehensible. [. . .] with this interpretation [of evil as sin] the essence of evil comes to light more clearly, even if in a quite determined direction. But evil is not to be reduced to sin and cannot be grasped under the heading of sin

alone. To the extent that our interpretation is attached to the real fundamental metaphysical question, the question of Being, it is not in the shape of sin that we question evil, but it is in the optic of the essence and truth of Being that we seek to situate it. And by that very fact it also appears, in mediate fashion, that the ethical horizon does not suffice to conceive of evil and that, much more than this, ethics and morality only aim, on the contrary, to legislate with a view to fixing the attitude to be adopted faced with evil, in the sense of the victory to be won against it, of the rejection or the diminishing of evil" (*Schelling*, p. 175 [p. 146]).

6. Even when, in *The Letter on Humanism* for example, these same heroes are mutually reinforcing in their opposition to "metaphysics," to the metaphysics of will or that which "thinks man on the basis of *animalitas*" and not "in the direction of his *humanitas*." "The body of man is something essentially other than an animal organism. The error of biologism is not overcome by the fact of adding the soul to the corporeal reality (*dem Leiblichen*) of man, and spirit to this soul, and to spirit the existential character, and by proclaiming louder than ever the high value of spirit" [trans. Frank A. Capuzzi, in *Basic Writings*, pp. 193–242 (p. 204)].

7. See what was said above about height, direction, and erection (p. 36). To avoid once again any simple or unilateral assignation, one could also cite Emmanuel Levinas: "The problem in each of the paragraphs on which we are commenting at present consists in reconciling the humanity of men and women with the hypothesis of a spirituality of the masculine, the feminine being not its correlative but its corollary, feminine specificity or the difference of the sexes which it announces not being situated from the outset at the level [*hauteur*] of the constitutive oppositions of Spirit. An audacious question: how can the equality of the sexes result from the priority of the masculine?" ("Et Dieu créa la femme," in *Du sacré au saint* [Paris: Minuit, 1977], p. 141). I have quoted and interpreted this passage in "En ce moment même dans cet ouvrage me voici," in *Psyché*, p. 115. This interpretation is also concerned with the questions of quotation marks, ashes, and the psyche in Levinas.

8. See for example what is said of discord (*Zwietracht*), of "distinction" as a minting (character), and the about-turn as "*Umschlag*" (*Schelling . . .*, pp. 215–17 [pp. 177–79]).

9. See "Comment ne pas parler."